VICTORY
THROUGH SURRENDER

A COLLAGE OF FAITH-BUILDING INSPIRATIONAL MESSAGES AND WISDOM NUGGETS

BY:
DR. RAYMOND P. FINDLATER

Copyright © 2013 by Dr. Raymond P. Findlater

Victory through Surrender
A collage of faith-building inspirational messages and wisdom nuggets
by Dr. Raymond P. Findlater

Printed in the United States of America

ISBN 9781626979871

All rights reserved solely by the author. The author guarantees all contents are original and do not infringe upon the legal rights of any other person or work. No part of this book may be reproduced in any form without the permission of the author. The views expressed in this book are not necessarily those of the publisher.

Unless otherwise indicated, Bible quotations are taken from
The Holy Bible, International Standard Version (ISV) © 2012
The Holy Bible, New International Version (NIV) © 2011
The Holy Bible, New Living Translation (NLT) © 2007
The Holy Bible, King James Version (KJV) © 2003
The Holy Bible, English Standard Version (ESV) © 2001
The Holy Bible, God's Word ® Translation © 1995

www.xulonpress.com

CONTENTS

INTRODUCTION ix
DEDICATION xi
ACKNOWLEDGMENTS xiii

CHAPTER 1: SURRENDER 15
    We are His righteousness even in the struggle
    Jesus is the only way out
    Time for sanctification
    Let's maintain our focus
    Lord, take full control today
    Are you willing to give up everything for Christ?
    The Lord desires that we be led by His Spirit
    This is no time to sit on the fence; you're either in or out
    We walk by faith
    Our reasonable service
    Grace through faith—nothing more nothing less
    Do you need a change?
    Lord, we are thirsty!
    Thus says the Lord
    Stay focused and let God do the rest
    Stay in the word; use the word
    Allow the Spirit of the Lord to take over
    Let the redeemed of the Lord say so
    Are you fit for the kingdom of God?
    What do you do when you don't know what to do?

God demands obedience; and any "but" after his command to us spells rebellion
Can you wait just a little longer?

CHAPTER 2: MATTER OF THE HEART 47
What's the one thing you desire most?
Cut them loose (put them out)
From knowledge to understanding
Let your light shine brightly; love one another
Have you received the promised Comforter/Counselor?
Do your words give life?
A scriptural, godly perspective
Your enemy is afraid; it's time to reclaim your stuff
Tell your enemy "It's all good"

CHAPTER 3: GOD LOVES SINNERS (DO YOU?) ... 67
Are you ready?
Father, forgive them
Have you been washed?
Have you met the Lord?
Pray for our adversaries
God's love versus the Jonah syndrome
What must I do to be saved?

CHAPTER 4: WHO IS HE AND WHAT IS HE TO YOU? 85
Jesus, name above every other name
We worship you, Jesus!
Where would I be without the Lord?
The reason for our hope
Where does the need for God fit into our "Hierarchy of Needs"?
True worshippers
The world needs our salt today
Who do you present to the world?
Can you see Him in the storm?
I don't have to see to believe

Contents

If we lose our life, we save it—one of the paradoxes of faith in Christ
"But as for me and my house"
Time to move over to Faith-ville
Following Christ
Let's become the unified Body of Christ
Are you equipped to respond appropriately?
My God is real
Lord, send laborers
We are very special to Him
Call upon Jesus today

CHAPTER 5: OTHER WISDOM NUGGETS........109
To live for Jesus Christ is to live by faith
Let's be productive, fruitful believers
What kind of children are we raising?
Whose report do you believe?
Have a thankful day
Thank you, Lord
Are you stressed out trying to be righteous?
Are your dreams big enough to attract dream-killers?
Be cautious
Be encouraged; there will be a time of joy and gladness
Let's be cheerful givers
God's word is enough to make us wise
Do not fall for their tricks
How much do you need God?
Don't lose sight of the vision (no pun intended)
Go forth and be strong in the Lord
God has promised mercy
God will teach us to profit when He leads
Accept what Jesus did on the cross and become the righteousness of God
The word of God is sweet
"Nothing can separate us from God's love"
Guided by truth

We are shining lights
We are triumphant
Overcomers
Have you overstayed your welcome in a certain season of your walk?
He's bringing us out
Let's praise and adore Him!
Set apart
Let's look to God for renewed strength today
Our God reigns
Persevere in prayer
It's good to serve the Lord
It's midnight
If you need a touch from the Lord today, pray with me
Let's drink from the Lord and be filled with His Spirit today
Enter into God's quiet rest
Like King Solomon, we should ask for wisdom
Walk in truth
Lord you are amazing, and I thank you!
Haven't I said that all things are possible? Only believe; the word of God cannot lie
Only worshipers will receive the rain
Legitimate reasons to boast
Our deliverance is wrapped up in praise
Persecution and suffering
Power to be witnesses
Speak, Lord
Preaching Christ crucified may sound foolish to some but …
Revive us and our land again, O Lord
Right thinking
Say Amen
Lord, by Your Spirit, shine through us today
Speaking and hearing as the learned
Strength and peace
Take time to know the Lord

Contents

Thank God for the Blood of Jesus
Thank the Lord for His word
Thank the Lord for Mercy!
Thank you Lord
Thanks and praise
The danger has passed and your deliverance is here
The Lord hears only the righteous
The Lord is always near when we need Him
Let's give God the glory that's rightfully His
The Lord will never disappoint those who trust Him
The word of God will sustain us
A day is coming when God shall reign in our favor forever
There is a ram in the bush for somebody; your Jehovah-Jireh has provided
There is power in prayer
Time to leave those idols behind and get fired up for God
Today is the day of salvation
Trust God and He will deliver
Get rid of that prideful spirit now!
We are free
We are made new in Christ
Praise the Lord, we are not forgotten
We are priests of God; let's wear our mantle well
We are standing on a sure foundation
We can do it
We have been given spiritual gifts by the Holy Spirit
We need to change because God does not
We need right living in the church, even under grace
Welcome His presence
What do you see?
The oracles of God
Your situation only needs a word from God
Benediction and blessing

REFERENCES 167

Introduction

> "To all who are victorious, who obey me to
> the very end, I will give authority."
> Revelation 2:26

Following the Lord requires obedience to the word of God and those spiritual promptings from the Holy Spirit we either choose to follow or ignore based on whether we think they make sense, whether they meet standards buried deep in the reservoir of our prior knowledge, or whether the end result of our obedience is implicit, fully certified, and guaranteed. We engage a line of reasoning in which to follow or not to follow predicated on whether we can reasonably deduce that in the final analysis victory will be a foregone conclusion. But a cursory glance at the inspired word of God, from Genesis to Revelation, suggests that victory comes through the unrestricted, uncompromising, singular-minded adherence to the guidance and direction of the Holy Spirit.

Many icons of the Old Testament including Abraham, King Saul, and King David and his son, Solomon (to name a few) have at one time or another veered away from the required directives and have tried to expedite God's plan, kept the spoils, committed murder and adultery, and bowed to false gods. In the case of Abraham, Israel and the world have inherited a half brother whose goal in life is the destruction of

Israel as a nation and the unleashing of terror on the Western world. King Saul's disobedience and defiance of God's order to destroy Amalek made him a reject in the eyes of the Lord and a pariah among his subjects. King David, dubbed a man after God's own heart, sent a trusted, loyal soldier to his death in order to steal the man's wife.

David's son, Solomon became king of Israel as a child and received a supernatural abundance of wisdom to discern right from wrong. Yet in spite of his access to a vast repository of knowledge and understanding, King Solomon had a weakness for strange women: marrying 300 and keeping a harem of 700 concubines. He later followed some of these foreign women in the worship of strange gods to the dismay of God Almighty.

This collage of inspirational messages and wisdom nuggets is not intended to magnify the failings of men or celebrate the weaknesses of God's people but to encourage believers on their journey through the maze of uncertainties, road blocks, trials and tribulations, temporary failings, and setbacks concomitant with the walk "to trust and obey" Jesus to the end. Therefore, if your goal is to experience daily victory, rule and reign with Christ then this book, *Victory through Surrender*, will provide inspiration and godly wisdom along the way.

Dedication

I am eternally grateful to my grandmother, Lillian Findlater whose love for God, wisdom, and kindness to me has left an indelible impression on my life. Her advice to "Trust God" still rings in my ears, long after she has gone on to be with the Lord. *Victory through Surrender* is dedicated to her memory.

Acknowledgments

First, all glory, honor, and praise to the King of Kings and Lord of Lords. I can say with all assuredness that in Him I live and move and have my being. This labor of love would not have been possible had it not been for the anointing of the Holy Spirit. He took me at my word when I made a promise to the Lord that if He helped me through the dissertation process of my doctoral program, then I would dedicate my life immediately following to the dissemination of the gospel of Jesus Christ.

Thank you, to my wife Audrey, daughters, Celene and Nadia, and son Ray 2, my grandchildren Alyssa, Jasmine, Ciera, Eric, and Jaden for their love and support. Thank you, Papa Earl and Mama Daisy, the two people responsible for bringing me into the world. I would be remiss not to mention my other family and friends on the most popular social networking site, who have read, commented, and encouraged me to compile and publish in book form some of their favorite messages and wisdom nuggets.

To all my extended family across the globe, thank you and much love. Last but not least, kudos to my editing assistant Christina Tilus for her help in organizing the manuscript in an order suited for submission.

Chapter One

SURRENDER

James 4:7 "Submit yourselves therefore to God. Resist the devil, and he will flee from you."

Most of us would like to experience victory in our lives on a consistent basis. We would like to celebrate, testify, and sing praises to the Lord for every milestone that has been achieved, mountain conquered, and each exit from valley experiences. Every child of God, at one time or another wants to taste and indulge the sweet aroma of a victorious event. For example, the implacable supervisor or boss gets transferred to another section or department after much intercession. The meddling co-worker accepts the gift of salvation and is now easy to get along with, after much intense prayer. Maybe the uncaring, reckless husband or wife relents under many months, even years of supplication in the midnight hour to the throne of grace. The mortgage company finally decides to modify that high interest loan, making the monthly payments more manageable just prior to final foreclosure action. If those scenarios don't apply, how about that child support payment that finally arrived at a time when the kids needed shoes, the car note was due, and hope was almost lost? Oh, we can't forget the immense sense of victory one feels when the drug-infested streets have coughed-up that prodigal child after what seemed to be an endless agonizing wait, trusting God for his/her return home.

Yes, we all seek victory over all those trials and tribulations we face on a daily basis, but quite often we forget one small detail in our journey. Child of God, if we should look back over the colorful canvases of our lives, it will have become very evident that those major victories over the enemy of our peace and tranquility came through a passage called surrender. Amen! If you are a believer facing unspeakable turmoil or besieged by issues that only God can solve right now, there could be only one small but vital detail keeping you from basking in the joyous, sweet aromatic essence of victory—surrender. The word of the Lord is saying at this moment in your life: it's time to surrender.

Before we travel any further on this passage called surrender it will be necessary to (1) define the term by exploring what it means to surrender; (2) introduce who needs to surrender; (3) answer why one needs to surrender; (4) find out when it's time to surrender; (5) discover where one should surrender; and (6) how should we surrender?

What does it mean to surrender?

Let's take a brief glance over a crucial moment in American and Japanese history: on September 2, 1945 Japan surrendered in Tokyo Bay. They had launched an attack against the United States of America at Pearl Harbor, Hawaii on December 7, 1941 and as a result, were the first recipients of the atomic bomb. Hence they needed no further persuasion to concede that it would be unwise to continue the fight and any lurking ambition toward maintaining an imperialist approach to international relations. Beaten and demoralized, the Japanese relinquished control of their country and internal affairs to a new dominant power. The lesser power has now become subservient to the greater power. Interestingly, Japan grew into an economic power because of their transfer of focus and resources from militarism to nation building and manufacturing for exportation.

Another definition of surrender can be found in the Complete Real Estate Encyclopedia by Denise L. Evans, JD–O William Evans, JD. (McGraw-Hill Companies). According to that source, surrender is "The cancellation of a lease or other contract by mutual agreement of the parties." So, we can summarize the definitions by saying that surrender is to give (something) over to the control or possession of another, usually under duress. For example, the teenager surrendered the keys to the car after five minutes of whining.

So far, we have stated that most people, especially we believers, want to live victorious lives. We said that as people of God, we should not forget one important detail in our quest for victory; and that is embodied in the word *surrender*. Also, we defined surrender and hopefully are in agreement that surrender means in the purest sense, to give something over to the control or possession of another and that we usually do so under duress or pressure.

Who needs to surrender?

This takes us to who are the parties involved in this transferring of control. It would be safe to say that everyone reading these pages, every believer, every sinner, including this writer must come to the truth that we need to surrender control to our Creator God or acquiesce under devil's onslaught. This takes us back to the text, James 4: 7, "Submit yourselves therefore to God. Resist the devil, and he will flee from you." Here the word of God makes it clear that we ought to relinquish control of our lives to God before we can even think about resisting the enemy, conquering that mountain, or adversity that is standing in our way. Of course, the One with the power and authority in this transaction is our God and King. Hallelujah! His name is Jesus. Our opponent and archenemy the devil lurks like a roaring lion especially for those who have not surrendered control to God.

For the sinner, in this instance the one who has not yet given his or her life over to Christ, the Holy Spirit is tugging at your heart, trying to draw you away from the control of the devil and bring you into fellowship with God. The word of God says in John chapter 3 and verse 16, "For God so loved the world, that he gave his only Son, that whosoever believes in him should not perish but have eternal life." Romans 6:23 declares that "the wages of sin is death, but the free gift of God is eternal life in Christ Jesus our Lord." If you do not know the Lord and have not turned over your life to Him, now is the time to be reconciled with God and inherit eternal life. Everyone needs to surrender, whether it's for salvation or for other victories that only God can provide.

Let's recap what we have talked about thus far. We have defined the what, by stating the definition of surrender as "to give something over to the control of another." We said God requires that believers submit or surrender; that sinners need to surrender to escape eternal damnation and receive eternal life. We stated further that the devil is our main enemy and that God wants control over our lives.

Why do we need to surrender?

This takes us to a more detailed discussion of the reasons why surrender is vital to our survival and ultimate victory. We know from history that the Japanese were overpowered militarily, which led to their surrender. But why do believers need to surrender? We know from scripture that sinners need to be reconciled with God and that they need to accept the free gift of salvation by faith in Christ to escape eternal damnation and obtain eternal life. But believers are saved people; we have the Holy Spirit operating in our lives. Surrender? Yes, the word of God admonishes all believers to submit (which means surrender).

Let's face it friends, our own efforts have been futile against the enemy. Half-hearted, infrequent prayers, hours of television, combined with a lack of meditation on the word of God have brought little or no results in terms of victory. Nothing positive seems to be happening; in fact, the battle has gotten hotter and frustration has grown heavier. On the other hand, you have prayed every prayer and quoted every scripture pertaining to prosperity and success in life but to no avail. Here are just four of the many reasons why a child of God may need to surrender especially, when times are tough:

(1) Mind Renewal

Are you living a life that is in conformity with the will of God? Or, are you living a Christian life on church day but a carnal one during the rest of the week? The word of God teaches in Romans 12:2, "Do not be conformed to this world, but be transformed by the renewal of your mind, that by testing you may discern what is the will of God, what is good and acceptable and perfect." We have heard it said over and over that God does not bless mess. We all need to surrender our minds to God. Let go of the world system. Give control over to the all wise, all powerful, and omnipresent God. Second Corinthians 7:1 reads, "Since we have these promises, beloved, let us cleanse ourselves from every defilement of body and spirit, bringing holiness to completion in the fear of God." We need to monitor the movies we watch (some are dark and ungodly), the music we listen to (many popular songs are loaded with demonic references, etc.), watch the company we keep (some folks will bring into your life depressing evil forces; others will influence you and your family in a negative way). Stay away from pornography and other addictive sins.

(2) Deliverance

Sometimes we are so far gone into the world system that our deliverance will come only after we confess our sins or faults one to another. First John 1:9 say that if we confess our sins, he is faithful and just to forgive our sins and cleanse us from all unrighteousness. But "wait a minute", you say, doesn't the word say that "there is therefore now no condemnation to them who are in Christ Jesus, who walk not after the flesh but after the Spirit." Why are you trying to condemn me? Well, my brother/sisters in Christ, you are partially correct. We are not condemned if we walk after the Spirit. The word states further, that "as many as are led by the spirit, they are the sons of God." That is why surrendering to the Spirit of Christ is so vitally important. When we present our bodies as living sacrifices, holy and acceptable to God, which is our spiritual worship, and refuse to be conformed to the world system, we place ourselves in the enviable position for deliverance—for whom the Lord sets free is free indeed.

(3) Love

One more reason why we need to surrender to the Spirit of God is to get the power to love. Usually, when things aren't going well we want to lash out at others. Especially at the ones who we have identified as being our enemies: the cause of our pain, discomfort, unhappiness at home, church, or out in the market place. Hate and resentment accumulate rapidly and some of us even pray like David to kill our enemies. But the Lord says in Luke 6:27–37 and I'll paraphrase: Love your enemies, do good to them that hate you, bless those who curse you, pray for them who abuse you; turn the other cheek to the one who strikes you, if the thief steals your cloak give him your tunic also. Give to everyone who begs from you; don't ask back for your stuff from the one who takes it from you. And do to others as you would have them do to you. Only total surrender to God can produce this particular attribute of the fruit of the Spirit. How else could you love an abusive husband or wife or the one who raped and committed horrendous atrocities against the ones you care about?

(4) Pruning

Maybe Father God is pruning you so that you will be able to bear more fruit. It is very easy for someone outside of your situation (troubled marriage, sickness in the family, loss of job, foreclosure on the home) to say that there may be sin in your life and that's the reason for your struggles and pain. That may or may not be the case. However, John 15:1–7 answers that dilemma,

> I am the true vine, and my Father is the vinedresser. Every branch in me that does not bear fruit he takes away, and every branch that does bear fruit he prunes, that it may bear more fruit. Already you are clean because of the word I have spoken to you. Abide in me, and I in you. As the branch cannot bear fruit by itself, unless it abides in the vine, neither can you, unless you abide in me. I am the vine; you are the branches. Whoever abides in me and I in him, he it is that bears much fruit, for apart from me you can do nothing.

Here you can see clearly that the Lord requires that we surrender to Him; that we abide in Him and He in us. In addition, from this passage we glean that struggles may arise because of not abiding, failure to surrender; or because God is allowing us to go through the unpleasant process of pruning.

I need to encourage someone at this point to hold on a little while longer, keep your will under submission to the will of God for your life right now. After the pruning, hallelujah, you will bear more fruit. You will see increase in the ministry, resolution of a complicated matter before the court, and healing in the family. Surrender to God and victory will be yours!

So far, we have defined surrender (the what); and said that everyone, the sinner and the believer must recognize their need for and total dependence on a sovereign God, through Jesus Christ our only lifeline. We discussed further, that the devil is our adversary who harasses and frustrates us and whose ultimate goal is to keep folks from being saved and keep the believer from reaching his or her destiny. We said also that a valid reason for surrendering, especially when going through tough times, is to bring about a renewal of the mind, a metamorphosis of sorts moving us from a state of conformity to the world to a higher level where we develop and maintain the mind of Christ. We said that surrender is essential for our deliverance; that love becomes a byproduct of surrendering to the Spirit of God; and that surrender is the only way to get victory while going through the pruning process. Surrendering to the will of God, giving up control of our lives and circumstances to Him, must occur at the earliest time possible. Delay could spell disaster both in the natural and spiritually.

When is it time to surrender?

Next, we need to know the appropriate time to surrender. The Japanese, to refer back to our earlier illustration, knew that after the decimation of Hiroshima and Nagasaki, any further attempt to defend against such a superior weapon would be foolhardy at best. Their only recourse, in terms of preventing total annihilation, was to surrender. People of God, let me ask you one question, what will it take to bring you to your knees, in total surrender to God? Father God has said in His word that He is a Spirit, and we should worship Him in Spirit and in truth. Let's forget about ourselves right now and bless the Lord. Let us surrender to Him; give all our cares, give all our ambitions, give Him all our fears, and take up our cross and follow Jesus. Let's crucify the flesh. Now is the time!

I hear the word of the Lord saying in Matthew 11:28–30,

> Come unto me, all who labor and are heavy laden, and I will give you rest. Take my yoke upon you, and learn of me, for I am gentle and lowly in heart, and you will find rest for your souls. My yoke is easy, and my burden is light.

Where do we surrender?

One may surrender to the Lord God anywhere because He sees us no matter where we are located, regardless of the dire straits in which we may have found ourselves. Father God said in Jeremiah 33:3 "Call unto me and I will answer thee and shew thee great and mighty things that thou knowest not." Space and time are irrelevant boundaries to the Almighty God. The Lord will meet us anywhere, in the church, in our bedroom, in the bar, or in the deepest pit of sin. Call on the Lord whereever you are right now, friend. Tough situations sometimes demand drastic measures to reach a proper solution.

When was the last time you just layed at the foot of the cross and bared your soul to the Lord? The songwriter wrote: "At the cross at the cross where I first saw the light and the burden of my heart rolled away; it was there by faith I received my sight and now I am happy all the day." Do you remember how happy you felt when you first got saved? The Lord desires that we come back to the source of joy because the joy of the Lord is our strength. It's time to surrender, be restored; and get back your joy.

How do we surrender?

During alter calls at a Billy Graham crusade the choir usually sang "Just as I am without one plea but that thy blood was shed for me." The point is that we should come just as we are with a broken and a contrite heart (Psalm 51:17). The unsaved should approach the Lord with this prayer: Father God, I repent of every sin that has separated me from you, and I confess that Jesus Christ is Lord. I believe in my heart that God raised Him from the dead. Thank you Lord for saving me, in the name of Jesus! I believe that if you didn't know the Lord and you prayed that prayer, you are saved.

If a believer desires restoration, wants to be set free he or she must understand that God requires that total submission; He asks that we come to Him and worship Him in Spirit and truth. It would be unwise to think that we can hold back anything from the One who sees everything. God looks deep into the heart to find sincerity and truth. Surrendering to God is to "come clean," to forsake our own efforts; to admit that our way is not working, and that we need God's divine intervention. The Bible says in Philippians 2:8 that Jesus was obedient even unto the cross; and God expects that kind of surrender from us as well.

Suffice it to say that victory comes through surrender. There is a popular phrase in Christian church circles that encourages us to "Let go and let God." In other words, give the control to God. We have two options: (1) fight to near-annihilation like the Japanese regrettably did, or (2) volunteer the reins to God while there is still time. Surrender will renew our mind, bring deliverance, fill our heart with love again, and allow us to go through the pruning process with patience and the knowledge that we are being prepared to bear more fruit. Here are some scriptures for your research and study: Psalm 1:1–3; 2 Timothy 3:12; 2 Peter 3:11; Galatians 2:20; 1 John

3:2–3; 2 Corinthians 5:17; Romans 5:1–21; Isaiah 26:3; John 16:33; Jeremiah 29:11; Job 22:23–27; Proverbs 3:1–4

Our day of Victory

I don't know what your personal challenges are at this moment in time but you can rest assured that a survey of the folks in your neighborhood or anywhere in the world for that matter would reveal that "The temptations in your life are no different from what others experience. And God is faithful. He will not allow the temptation to be more than you can stand. When you are tempted, he will show you a way out so that you can endure" (1 Corinthians 10:13). Here are a few scripture verses that speak to the matter in terms that are clearly God's way of achieving lasting victory in our daily walk:

- James 4:7 "Submit yourselves therefore to God. Resist the devil, and he will flee from you." Note that, the devil is not afraid of you in your own strength but he is powerless against the individual who is wrapped up in God.
- John 15:1–7 "I am the true vine, and my Father is the vinedresser. Every branch in me that does not bear fruit he takes away, and every branch that does bear fruit he prunes, that it may bear more fruit. Already you are clean because of the word that I have spoken to you. Abide in me, and I in you. As the branch cannot bear fruit by itself, unless it abides in the vine, neither can you, unless you abide in me. I am the vine; you are the branches. Whoever abides in me and I in him, he it is that bears much fruit, for apart from me you can do nothing." Friend, we will be successful believers on the battle field for the Lord, if and only if, we remain connected to Christ.

- 1 Peter 5:6–10 "Humble yourselves, therefore, under the mighty hand of God so that at the proper time he may exalt you, casting all your anxieties on him, because he cares for you. Be sober-minded; be watchful. Your adversary the devil prowls around like a roaring lion, seeking someone to devour. Resist him, firm in your faith, knowing that the same kinds of suffering are being experienced by your brotherhood throughout the world. And after you have suffered a little while, the God of all grace, who has called you to his eternal glory in Christ, will himself restore, confirm, strengthen, and establish you."

I encourage you to hold on to "God's unchanging hand" and be humble, in spite of the situation you are facing at the moment. Seek the Lord in whatever you do and as Proverbs 3:5 suggests, "Trust in the Lord with all thine heart; and lean not unto thine own understanding." Finally, Psalm 37:5 advises, "Commit thy way unto the Lord; trust also in him; and he shall bring *it* to pass." As you can see, child of God, we get our victory through surrender.

We are His righteousness even in the struggle

Romans 7:19–21, 24 says, "For the good that I would I do not: but the evil which I would not, that I do. Now if I do that I would not, it is no more I that do it, but sin that dwelleth in me. I find then a law, that, when I would do good, evil is present with me. O wretched man that I am! Who shall deliver me from the body of this death?"

Friend, we are caught in a clash between a desire to serve the law of God and a strong inclination to serve the law of sin. It's a struggle that will cause us to feel dejected and defeated, especially in instances when we have yielded to the flesh or succumbed to the thing we know to be incongruous with the word of God. If you are in that place right now, take heart, child of God. There is a way out of this dilemma. We must surrender to the Spirit of Christ. According to Romans 8:1–2, "There is therefore now no condemnation to them which are in Christ Jesus, who walk not after the flesh, but after the spirit. For the law of the Spirit of life in Christ Jesus hath made me free from the law of sin and death.

Christian, it's time to recognize that we are no longer in the flesh, but in the Spirit, because the Spirit of God dwells in us. Further, if the Spirit of Christ resides in us, the body is dead because of sin; but the Spirit is life because of righteousness (Romans 8:9–10). Freedom comes when we have resolved to follow the leading of the Spirit of God and receive the power to crucify the deeds of the flesh. Finally brethren, no matter how intense the struggle, we must never forget that we are heirs of God and joint-heirs with Christ. Praise the Lord!

Jesus is the only way out

John 3:16–17 says,
For God so loved the world that he gave his only begotten Son, that whosoever believeth in him should not perish, but have everlasting life. [17] For God sent not his Son into the world to condemn the world but that the world through him might be saved.

We are living in an age in which knowledge has increased exponentially, technological advancements have climbed to unprecedented heights, and man's thirst for pleasure has outgrown his ability to satisfy it, in spite of the ingenious methods being employed. There seems to be a huge hole, an empty space, in the heart of so many people—a chasm that man-centered attempts at filling have proved unsuccessful. What is the cause of this malaise? Isaiah 59:2–3 declares

Your iniquities have been barriers between you and your God, and your sins have hidden his face from you so that he does not hear. 3) For your hands are defiled with blood, and your fingers with iniquity; your lips have spoken lies, your tongue mutters wickedness.

Is there a way out?

There is only one way out of this "great divide," and His name is Jesus (John 14:6). Until we have been reconciled with God through Jesus Christ—brought back into a right relationship with our Creator—we will continue to lead unfulfilled lives (Romans 5:10; 2 Corinthians 5:18–20). Beloved, if you have this unquenchable need deep down inside that nothing seems to satisfy, try Jesus. Romans 10:9 states, "If you confess with your mouth that Jesus is Lord and believe in your heart that God raised him from the dead, you will be saved." Jesus is the only way out.

Time for sanctification

Joshua 3:5 says, "And Joshua said unto the people, sanctify yourselves: for tomorrow the Lord will do wonders among you."

There comes a time when we have to separate ourselves from the daily routine, the things that occupy our thought processes and affections in order to get ready for the next level in God. Nothing must distract us or steal our focus because the Lord is about to do something new, and we can't afford to miss the display of divine intervention, designed to show forth His glory. We are going to an unfamiliar place with bigger challenges, huge responsibilities, and giant-sized obstacles requiring a different mindset. We'll need a larger measure of faith that pleases our wonderful, miracle-working God and a desire to worship Him in spirit and in truth. Is your heart ready to receive the secrets reserved for the servants of

God? Can you hear the still, small voice of the Holy Spirit providing instructions on how to traverse your Jordan River on dry (holy) ground?

The following scripture verses address the need for sanctification:

> Titus 2:11–14 "For the grace of God that brings salvation has appeared to all men, teaching us that, denying ungodliness and worldly lusts, we should live soberly, righteously, and godly in the present age, looking for the blessed hope and glorious appearing of our great God and Savior Jesus Christ, who gave Himself for us, that He might redeem us from every lawless deed and purify for Himself His own special people, zealous for good works."

> 1 Peter1:13–16 "Therefore gird up the loins of your mind, be sober, and rest your hope fully upon the grace that is to be brought to you at the revelation of Jesus Christ; as obedient children, not conforming yourselves to the former lusts, as in your ignorance; but as He who called you is holy, you also be holy in all your conduct."

Friends, let's sanctify ourselves today; "Looking unto Jesus the author and finisher of our faith; who for the joy that was set before him endured the cross, despising the shame, and is set down at the right hand of the throne of God" (Hebrews 12:2). We'll never get to the next level in God with the same sinful mindset.

Let's maintain our focus

> The eyes of the LORD search the whole earth in order to strengthen those whose hearts are fully committed to him. What a fool you have been! From now on you will be at war. (2 Chronicles 16:9, NLT)

In 2 Chronicles 14, Asa, King of Judah, rid the nation of their false gods and dedicated himself and the people to the true and living God. They came under attack by a ferocious million-man-strong army with three hundred chariots. Asa sought the Lord and relied totally on Him for help. The Lord intervened and the enemy was defeated. In 2 Chronicles 15:2, the word of the Lord reminded Asa, "The Lord is with you, while ye be with him; and if ye seek (desire) him, he will be found (near) of you; but if ye forsake (leave) him, he will forsake you."

Oded the prophet continued by reminding Asa that when the people kept their focus on God, He delivered nations into their hands. In other words, the God of Israel was more than able to perform wars on the behalf of His people and give them victory, regardless of the odds against them. The prophet concluded by telling Asa to "Be strong therefore, and let not your hands be weak; for your work shall be rewarded." There was a great revival in Jerusalem, as the nation repented and turned to the Lord, but by the time we get to Chapter 16, Judah came under threat of attack from outlaw Israel, ruled at the time by King Baasha.

Out of fear, King Asa of Judah sought the assistance of Benhadad, king of Syria. Unbelievable! How could a man, after having received such encouraging promises from the Lord, turn to another source for help? But isn't that what we do, our modus operandi? One problem, one attack, a scary moment and we resort to our natural inclination—to seek the arm of flesh for support. How many men and women of God violate God's word when faced with the simplest of challenges to his or her faith?

Why do we forget the promises of God, including the one that says "The Lord is with you, while ye be with him?" How could anyone ignore a word that warns "If ye seek him, he will be found of you; but if ye forsake him, he will forsake you?" Folks, we are servants of the Most High God; can't we hear Jeremiah 32:27 ringing in our ears, "Is anything too hard for God?" We have the example of the Apostle Paul, who encourages us with his persevering spirit in 2 Corinthians 12:10, "Therefore I take pleasure in infirmities, in reproaches, in necessities, in persecutions, in distresses for Christ's sake: for when I am weak, then am I strong."

Our text indicates that God is watching to see who is committed to Him and promises to provide strength in our weakest moments. If we take our eyes off the Lord, our source of strength, then we are left vulnerable to the enemies of our peace. Friend, we can't afford to lose our focus now, "For all of God's promises have been fulfilled in Christ with a resounding "Yes!" And through Christ, our "Amen" (which means "Yes") ascends to God for his glory" (2 Corinthians 1:20).

Lord, take full control today

Colossians 3:17 says, "And whatever you do, whether by speech or action, do everything in the name of the Lord Jesus, giving thanks to God the Father through him."

Lord I surrender my body, soul and spirit to your will today—let my wants, desires, and thoughts be in conformity to your wants, desires, and will for my life. Let me speak as the oracle of the Lord and bring edification to the hearers this day, according to your word. Father God, lead, direct, and orchestrate everything I do by your Spirit, in the name above every other name, Jesus the Christ (Yeshua Ha-Mashiach). Thank you, Lord!

Are you willing to give up everything for Christ?

Mark 8:34–36: "Then he called his disciples and the crowd to come over and listen. "If any of you wants to be my follower," He told them, "you must put aside your selfish ambition, shoulder your cross, and follow me. If you try to keep your life for yourself, you will lose it. But if you give up your life for my sake and for the sake of the Good News, you will find true life. And how do you benefit if you gain the whole world but lose your own soul in the process?"

While serving in the military during the 1991 Desert Storm campaign in the Middle East, I overheard a conversation between a few young troops. The gist of their discussion was that they had signed up to enjoy free travel around the world, educational benefits, and other perks that were a part of the benefits package provided to American servicemen and women during peace time. However, the young warriors had not bargained for the inconveniences associated with being an American fighting machine. They were upset and devastated at the thought of actually being sent into the desert to fight a war and possibly losing their lives or limbs. Reality had visited them on the battlefield; the cost of their enlistments, they discovered, was not cheap.

Like those young servicemen and women, many Christians assumed that when they invited Christ into their lives their troubles would have disappeared and life would be like walking down the Streets of Gold. Some believe, based on the for-profit gospel being bandied about in certain circles that following Jesus means a life down easy street, with possessions untold. Others think that sitting in church surrounded by friendly faces, in cushiony, warm pews and imbibing the sweet stew of feel-good preaching are inherent benefits of the great commission. Please don't mention trials and tribulations because those who wish to "gain the whole world" will brand you as a preacher of doom and gloom.

Very few have been told that following the Lord meant a life of sacrifice, self-denial, hardships, uncertainty, and total obedience to the leading of the Holy Spirit. Someone should have told them that in this walk, giving up one's life for the sake of Christ and the Good News is the only path by which one finds "true life." Child of God, we need to understand that following Jesus, though costly, paves the way to glory; while seeking after and gaining everything the world has to offer ultimately will result in the loss of our souls. Are you willing to give up everything for Christ?

The Lord desires that we be led by His Spirit

Romans 8:7 says, "Because the carnal mind is enmity against God: for it is not subject to the law of God, neither indeed can be."

Friend, there was a time when I thought that grace forgave my willful disobedience of God's word; and gladly pleased my fleshly desires, as long as no one got hurt and I was not found out. Well, why not? Doesn't the word say in Romans 8:1 that "there is therefore now no condemnation to them who are in Christ Jesus"? Little did I know that my "carnal mind" was "enmity against God."

Like so many Christians, I was exercising my privileges under grace and had become, as Pastor Marvin Jackson of The River of Life Christian Center of Orlando, Florida puts it, "desensitized to sin." But the word of God is teaching us today that we who are in Christ Jesus ought to allow the Spirit of God to lead us; "For as many as are led by the Spirit of God, they are the sons of God" (Romans 8:14).

Child of God, the carnal mind "is not subject to the law of God," therefore, "they that are in the flesh cannot please God." In Galatians 6:7–8, the Apostle Paul wrote "Be not deceived; God is not mocked: for whatsoever a man soweth, that shall he also reap. For he that soweth to his flesh shall of the flesh reap corruption (death); but he that soweth to the Spirit shall of the Spirit reap life everlasting."

Father God, your word says that if we confess our sins you are faithful and just to forgive us of those sins and cleanse us from all unrighteousness (1 John 1:9); now, forgive us of our willful disobedience of your word, in Jesus' name. May the Spirit of God lead us today.

This is no time to sit on the fence; you're either in or out

> For we have not followed cunningly devised fables, when we made known unto you the power and coming of our Lord Jesus Christ, but were eyewitnesses of his majesty. For he received from God the Father honour and glory, when there came such a voice to him from the excellent glory, this is my beloved Son, in whom I am well pleased. And this voice which came from heaven we heard, when we were with him in the holy mount. We have also a more sure word of prophecy; whereunto ye do well that ye take heed, as unto a light that shineth in a dark place, until the day dawn, and the day star arise in your hearts: Knowing this first that no prophecy of the scripture is of any private interpretation. For the prophecy came not in old time by the will of man: but holy men of God spake as they were moved by the Holy Ghost (2 Peter 1:16–21).

Maybe you are an intellectual who has been trying to figure out if all that you've been taught in Sunday school has any merit. Your critical thinking skills have gotten the better of you, and now you are wavering. Maybe you have studied the theory of evolution or have become a Postmodernist thinker, skeptical of any absolutes, sitting on the proverbial fence, trying to process all this "Jesus stuff"—salvation by grace through faith.

The Apostle Peter is saying that he and many others were eyewitnesses to the life and times of Jesus. In addition, the prophets of old proclaimed the acceptable day of the Lord through and under the anointing of the Holy Spirit of God. They spoke of a very real God and a Savior who loved us so much that He died for our sins. His desire is that we might live eternally with Him—if only we confess Jesus as our Lord and believe in our hearts that God raised Him from the dead.

The text is encouraging us to follow those things that we were taught in the word of God and hold fast to the teachings of our Lord Jesus because He is the only true, living Savior and Lord of all. Friend, by faith return to your first love (Jesus) and ask Him to show you how real He is! You will not be disappointed. I adjure you, look around and pay attention to the signs; prophecies are being fulfilled all around us. This is no time to sit on the fence; you're either in or out.

We walk by faith

Second Corinthians 5:7 (KJV) says "For we walk by faith and not by sight:"

Friends, as we face the world and its challenges today, remember that this is not our home. We have an eternal future pending with the Holy One of Israel, our God and King. Therefore, while the lost of this world mistakenly think that this life is all that there is to living, we know that to be present in this body is to be absent from the Lord and to be absent from the body is to be present with the Lord (2 Corinthians 5:6, 8). Hence, in the language of the New Living Translation, "That is why we live by believing and not by seeing." We look for a city "whose builder and maker is God" (Hebrews 11:10).

Our reasonable service

Romans 12:1 (NLT), "And so, dear brothers and sisters, I plead with you to give your bodies to God because of all he has done for you. Let them be a living and holy sacrifice—the kind he will find acceptable. This is truly the way to worship him."

Father God, help all of us who profess Jesus, as Savior and Lord to recognize that our lives belong solely to you; and that everything about us, especially our bodies, should be presented as "a living and holy sacrifice" unto you. We ask for a renewing of our minds, a new way of thinking that would open our spiritual eyes to recognize what the will of God is and be able to walk in it. Unite us as one body in Christ and teach us how to function appropriately in our respective callings; using our gifts and talents for your glory. May we learn to appreciate your good and perfect will and not copy the ways of the world. This Lord, is our reasonable service to you, in Jesus' name.

Grace through faith—nothing more nothing less

Ephesians 2:8–9 "For by grace are ye saved through faith; and that not of yourselves: it is the gift of God; not of works, lest any man should boast."

There are many folks who have spent their entire lives trying to be good and righteous. Some have spent most of their lives obeying the commandments and following strict adherence to religious legalisms, hoping to please their leaders and be saved in the sight of God. However, as commendable as these personal attempts to reach God have been, the Prophet Isaiah says that all our righteousness is as filthy rags (Isaiah 64:6); and that smashes any individual effort to be good, every iota of self-righteousness, into nothingness.

The Apostle Paul, a man who had been a successful student of Judaic Law, a highly esteemed and zealous Pharisee prior to meeting Christ, admitted the irrelevance of his own righteousness and accomplishments compared to knowing and living for Jesus by faith. He wrote in Philippians 3:7–9,

> I once thought all of these things were so very important, but now I consider them worthless because

of what Christ has done. Yes, everything else is worthless when compared with the priceless gain of knowing Christ Jesus my Lord. I have discarded everything else, counting it all as garbage, so that I may have Christ; and become one with him. I no longer count my own goodness or my ability to obey God's law, but I trust Christ to save me. For God's way of making us right with himself depends on faith.

Friend, being saved is by grace through faith—nothing more, nothing less.

Do you need a change?

"Therefore if any man be in Christ, he is a new creature: old things are passed away; behold all things are become new" (2 Corinthians 5:17).

If you are tired of the kind of life you're living and desire real change, the Lord has got a good plan for your life (Jeremiah 29:11). To step into this promise of a new, superior lifestyle, first one must meet Jesus at Calvary's cross and accept Him as Savior and Lord. He will create in you a new heart; by his Spirit He will give you new reasons for living.

God is waiting on you, no matter how low or how high, regardless of how sinful or terrible your life may be right now. The Lord will meet you where you are and take you to the place you ought to be. Friend, do you need a change? Would you like to become a new creation in Christ and experience a new way of living?

Pray this prayer with me: Lord Jesus, you are Lord and I believe that you died and that God raised you from the dead. Come into my life and make me a new person. Amen.

Lord, we are thirsty!

John 4:13–14: "Jesus answered and said unto her, Whosoever drinketh of this water shall thirst again: But whosoever drinketh of the water that I shall give him shall never thirst; but the water that I shall give him shall be in him a well of water springing up into everlasting life."

We all, at one time or another, seek out our own means to satiate feelings of emptiness, loneliness, and the desire for love, in ways contrary to the plan of God for our lives. As a result, we go from bed to bed, spend our nights in smoky places, over-indulge in alcohol and drugs, even overeating to no avail. Like the adulterous woman in our text, many of us are trying to find that one fix, orgasm, or elixir that would remedy the seemingly unquenchable desire for total satisfaction.

The Rolling Stones, in their seminal contribution to the music world, sang: "I can't get no satisfaction," a phrase which has defined generations since time immemorial. Unfortunately, many professed "born-again" folks have seen their lives spiral out of control, as they search unsuccessfully for something more, for satisfaction. But Jesus is saying, come to the source of life, the one with everything necessary to fulfill all our desires.

Friend, if you are caught in an unpleasant web of attempts aimed at pacifying those uncontrollable cravings for gratification, there is a way out. Surrender to the Lord today; receive inside of you "a well of water springing up into everlasting life" and thirst no more. Let's pray! Father, our thirst for fulfillment has driven us into areas distant from your divine plan for our lives. Have mercy upon us, forgive us of our sins and cleanse us from all unrighteousness. Satisfy us with your living water; in the name of Jesus.

Thus says the Lord

Psalm 44:3 says "They did not conquer the land with their swords: it was not their own strength that gave them victory. It was by your mighty power that they succeeded; it was because you favored them and smiled on them.

Stop trying to force the issue. Haven't I said that "It is not by force nor by strength, but by my Spirit? (Zechariah 4:6). In the moment when you think not, a time when you least expect it, I will do a thing that will defy the odds against you. Then, they will know that the hand of the Lord did it. God alone will get the credit for your victory. Honor, glory and majesty to the name of the Lord!

Stay focused and let God do the rest

In Nehemiah 6:16, we read, "When our enemies and the surrounding nations heard about it, they were frightened and humiliated. They realized this work had been done with the help of our God."

We will not be deterred from our purpose. Like Nehemiah and the builders of the wall at Jerusalem, our focus will be on the assignment which the Lord has instructed us to finish. Tell your Sanballats and the rest of the scorners that "if God be for us, who can be against us?" (Romans 8:31). Today, our enemies and mockers have reason to fear because according to Isaiah 59:19, "So shall they fear the name of the LORD from the west, and his glory from the rising of the sun. When the enemy shall come in like a flood, the Spirit of the LORD shall lift up a standard against him."

As Moses declared to the people in Exodus 14:13, even so shall it be this day "… . .Fear ye not, stand still, and see the salvation of the Lord, which he will show to you to day: for the Egyptians whom ye have seen to day, ye shall see them again no more for ever." Hallelujah! The Psalmist proclaimed in Psalm 46:1–3 "God is our refuge and strength, a very present help in trouble. Therefore will not we fear, though the earth be removed, and though the mountains be carried into the midst of the sea; though the waters thereof roar and be troubled, though the mountains shake with the swelling thereof. Selah." Let them talk; only stay focused and let God do the rest.

Stay in the word; use the word

All scripture is inspired by God and is useful to teach us what is true and to make us realize what is wrong in our lives. It straightens us out and teaches us to do what is right. It is God's way of preparing us in every way, fully equipped for every good thing God wants us to do (2 Timothy 3:16–17).

Have you ever been down in spirit and came upon a verse or passage in the Bible that went, as it were, to the heart of the matter; a word that immediately lifted you into recovery? Remember that word you received that carried you through the stormy days? And what about the time when you weren't quite sure what direction to take and a word from the Psalms or Proverbs brought light and clarity? Then, there were days when you felt like engaging in what's expedient but not right, but the word of God, hidden in your heart, kept you from sinning.

The word of God, according to Ephesians 6:17 is "the sword of the Spirit." It is an offensive weapon, which when used appropriately will chase the adversary from your presence. Jesus used the scripture as a weapon against Satan when He was being tempted. Note that, the Lord prefaced each response to the tempter with the phrase "It is written" (Matthew 4). Likewise we need to be armed with the word of faith, which enables us to speak "thus says the Lord" to situations that would prevent us from doing the will of God.

Finally, the word furnishes the believer with the tools needed to gently teach those who oppose the truth and prepares us to give an answer to anyone who asks for a reason for our belief in Christ Jesus. Friend, the word prepares and equips us to do what God wants us to do. The Holy Scripture will make the simple person wise.

Allow the Spirit of the Lord to take over

My blessed friend, as you embark upon this new level of confrontation with your "great mountain," the word of the Lord of hosts rings loud and clear this morning: "Not by might, nor by power, but by my spirit" (Zechariah 4:6–7). By God's grace you shall witness the demonstration of the Spirit of the Lord, working on your behalf to move that gigantic obstacle out of your way. You have been expending your own might and power, with much frustration and very little success. It's now time to "let go" and allow the Spirit of the Lord to take over.

Let the redeemed of the Lord say so

Every child of God has something to thank the Lord for today. The Psalmist declares in Psalm 107:1–2, "O give thanks unto the Lord for he is good: for his mercy endureth for ever. Let the redeemed of the Lord say so, whom he hath redeemed from the hand of the enemy."

Are you one of the redeemed? The answer is yes if you have accepted Jesus Christ as Savior and Lord, and your sins have been washed away by His shed blood at Calvary. Yes, if you were once lost but now have been found; if you were blind, now you can see. Yes, if you have divorced yourself from the way of the evil one and are now walking in the righteousness of God through Jesus Christ.

Say yes, if Satan had you bound but Jesus set you free. Yes, if your hope and aspirations are to please the Lord and if the word of God sanctifies your heart and keeps you pure.

Yes, if you have chosen to allow the Holy Spirit of God to lead you into all truth. Say yes, if you are one of the redeemed.

The songwriter wrote: "Redeemed, how I love to proclaim it! Redeemed by the blood of the Lamb; Redeemed thro' His infinite mercy, His child, and forever I am." Let the redeemed of the Lord say so.

Are you fit for the kingdom of God?

Luke 9:62: "And Jesus said unto him, No man, having put his hand to the plough, and looking back, is fit for the kingdom of God."

Friend, being a field worker in the service of the Lord requires total dedication and selflessness. Our salvation is not just a badge of honor to be worn conveniently. Jesus has called us to take up His cross and follow him, to give up our own will for our heavenly Father's. We are sent out as lambs among wolves, stripped of our own usual means of survival, to be totally reliant on God (Luke 10:3–4). The believer thus becomes the representative of Christ in the highways and byways of life; preaching and teaching the gospel, healing the sick and casting out devils in the name of Jesus. Whether on a secular job or in full time ministry the commission is the same; to give hope to the hopeless, sight to the blind, light where there is darkness, and peace where there is turmoil.

The child of God gets no time off from service; his or her focus must always be on winning souls for the kingdom and the mantra is always "Here I am Lord, send me." Contrary to popular belief, the life of a follower of Christ is not always eating and drinking, making merry, and enjoying a lifetime of "material prosperity." One must be prepared to go through times of hardship and stiff opposition both in the natural and spiritually, although victory is guaranteed. To be on the frontline for Jesus demands that the servant of God spends significant time in prayer and fasting; studying the word of

God, and staying equipped to be able to stand against the wiles of the devil (Ephesians 6:11). In this service there is no turning back; it's forward march all the way, from glory to glory. Are you fit for the kingdom of God?

What do you do when you don't know what to do?

Mark 11:22 (NLT) says, "Then Jesus said to the disciples, "Have faith in God."

What do you do when you've preached a well-received message on faith, and the next day your innocent five year old grandchild screams and writhes in excruciating pain that goes unabated in spite of your desperate pleas to God? What do you do when sickle cell anemia mercilessly batters her fragile body, and your mind tells you that your faith is neither big enough nor strong enough to effect an immediate healing? Have faith in God and believe anyway (Hebrews 11).

What do you do when the woman you love tells you she doesn't love you anymore; or that man to whom you have given the best years of your life tells you that he has found someone new? What do you do when you have lived an exemplary life as a mate, but heartbreak and sadness knocks at the door of your love nest? Have faith in God and love anyway (1 Corinthians 13).

What do you do when the young people in your community have become instruments of destruction in the hands of the evil one, causing death and mayhem among themselves? What do you do when the seeds of drugs and sexually transmitted diseases ravage your neighborhood? What do you do when law enforcement officials and governmental representatives pay lip service to the suffering and hopelessness of their constituents? Have faith in God! Only the Lord is able to "Give us aid against the enemy, for the help of man is worthless" (Psalm 108:12).

What do you do when some men and women placed in charge of the spiritual well-being of the sheep turn out to be wolves in sheep's clothing? What do you do when those who should be wiping away your tears are the ones causing them? What do you do when the song and dance was just a tactic to hijack hard-earned wages and make the unscrupulous rich? Have faith anyway because there is a reward for righteousness; God is judge of the earth (Psalm 58:11).

Child of God, what do you do when you don't know what to do? Have faith in God.

> May the Lord bless you and keep you: May the Lord make His face shine upon you, and be gracious unto you: May the Lord lift up his countenance upon you and give you peace (Numbers 6:24).

God demands obedience, and any "but" after his command to us spells rebellion

> Now go and smite Amalek and utterly destroy all that they have, and spare them not; but slay man and woman, infant and suckling, ox and sheep, camel and ass. But Saul and the people spared Agag, and the best of the sheep, and the oxen, and of the fatlings, and the lamb, and all that was good, and would not utterly destroy them: but every thing that was vile and refuse, that they destroy utterly. (1 Samuel 15:3, 9)

Friend, never put a "but" after God's command to you. Saul's "but" landed him into a precarious place of rebellion against God. He thought that partial obedience would be good enough. However, verses 22 and 23 of the same chapter show that the Lord is not too excited about anything other than total adherence to his directives; consider our deviation from His word rebellion. That, God said, is as the sin of witchcraft.

To rebel against God's word is to reject Him, and if we reject our Lord he will likewise reject us. The consequences

Surrender

for our disobedience may be that missed promotion that we thought we could get achieve on our own terms, losing our ministry, and other eventualities that leave us chasing our tails like foolish dogs. The morale of the story in 1 Samuel is that God says what He means and means what He says; therefore, anything we do other than what are required places us in jeopardy of being passed over for the next level in God's kingdom.

Lord, have mercy on me, you, and all those who have lived in disobedience before the Most Holy God. Lord, thank you for mercy this day because we have sinned and come short of the glory of God. Wash us in the blood of the Lamb slain before the foundation of the world, in the name of Jesus.

Can you wait just a little longer?

Psalm 40:1–2: "I waited patiently for the Lord; and he inclined unto me, and heard my cry. 2) He brought me up out of a horrible pit, out of the miry clay, and set my feet upon a rock, and established my goings."

According to Webster's College Dictionary, wait is defined as "remaining inactive or in a state of repose, as until something expected happens." Child of God, I don't know the reason for your wait today but the question is Can you wait just a little longer? There is an old adage that suggests that good things come to those who wait, and most of us would agree with those words. But waiting can be exhausting, frustrating, and somewhat unbearable at times.

Usually, it's during this waiting period that folks get tired, weary, and tempted to let go of their plans and dreams. This is the season when some Christians decide that maybe God has forsaken them and they begin, tragically, to build their own sacred calves and do what they think is best for them. If you are tired of waiting today, Isaiah 40:31 declares "But those who wait on the Lord will find new strength. They will fly high like the eagles. They will run and not grow weary. They will walk and not faint."

Here are words of encouragement from the Psalmist David, a man who knew something about waiting, found in Psalm 37:34, "Wait on the Lord, and keep his way, and he shall exalt thee to inherit the land. . . ." My friend, it's vitally important to stay focused on God while you are waiting and "keep his way." Victory is closer than you think. Can you wait just a little longer?

Chapter Two

IT'S A MATTER OF THE HEART

"Create in me a clean heart, O God and
renew a right spirit in me."
Psalm 51:10

One does not have to be a medical professional to grasp the profound importance of the heart. The heart has been referred to as one of the most vital organs in the human body. The Psalmist, David addressed the condition of his 'heart' in Psalm 51 and in verse 10 asked God for a cleansing and a renewal of a right spirit within him. Thus, we know that he was not alluding to the natural heart within his chest but a heart that we will refer to as, for obvious reasons, the Bible heart. For this study we will review the following topics: What is the heart (in the natural and Bible heart), some common diseases, possible cures, protection, and nourishment.

What is the heart (in the natural)?

Your heart is a muscular organ that pumps blood to your body. Your heart is at the center of your circulatory system.

This system consists of a network of blood vessels, such as arteries, veins, and capillaries. These blood vessels carry blood to and from all areas of your body.

An electrical system controls your heart and uses electrical signals to contract the heart's walls. The walls contract and blood is pumped into your circulatory system. Inlet and outlet valves in your heart chambers ensure that blood flows in the right direction.

Your heart is vital to your health and nearly everything that goes on in your body. Without the heart's pumping action, blood can't move throughout your body. Your blood carries the oxygen and nutrients that your organs need to work well. Blood also carries carbon dioxide (a waste product) to your lungs so you can breathe it out.

A healthy heart supplies your body with the right amount of blood at the rate needed to work well. If disease or injury weakens your heart, your body's organs won't receive enough blood to work normally.

Some common diseases of the heart

There are numerous diseases associated with the heart but the most common heart disease is Coronary Heart Disease (CHD). If the flow of oxygen-rich blood to your heart muscle is reduced or blocked, angina (an-JI-nuh or AN-juh-nuh) or a heart attack can occur. Angina is chest pain or discomfort. It may feel like pressure or squeezing in your chest. The pain also can occur in your shoulders, arms, neck, jaw, or back. Angina pain may even feel like indigestion.

A heart attack occurs if the flow of oxygen-rich blood to a section of heart muscle is cut off. If blood flow isn't restored quickly, the section of heart muscle begins to die. Without quick treatment, a heart attack can lead to serious health problems or death. Over time, CHD can weaken the heart muscle and lead to heart failure and arrhythmias (ah-RITH-me-ahs).

Heart failure is a condition in which your heart can't pump enough blood to meet your body's needs. Arrhythmias are problems with the rate or rhythm of the heartbeat.

Possible cures

CHD is the most common type of heart disease. In the United States, CHD is the number one cause of death for both men and women. Lifestyle changes, medicines, and medical procedures can help prevent or treat CHD. These treatments may reduce the risk of related health problems. What happens when the heart disease becomes incurable? Death or transplant (means a new heart is donated by someone who died).

Protection and nourishment

- Get balanced diet, exercise, rest,
- have a balanced life,
- and get regular check-ups.

What is the Bible Heart?

"Kardia: 'the heart' (Eng., 'cardiac,' etc.), the chief organ of physical life ('for the life of the flesh is in the blood,' Lev. 17:11), occupies the most important place in the human system. By an easy transition the word came to stand for man's entire mental and moral activity, both the rational and the emotional elements. In other words, the heart is used figuratively for the hidden springs of the personal life. "The Bible describes human depravity as in the "heart," because sin is a principle which has its seat in the center of man's inward life, and then "defiles" the whole circuit of his action, (Matthew 15:19, 20). On the other hand, Scripture regards the heart as the sphere of Divine influence, Romans 2:15; Acts 15:9.... The heart, as lying deep within, contains 'the hidden man,' 1 Peter 3:4, the real man. It represents the true character but conceals it" (J. Laidlaw, in Hastings' Bible Dictionary) Expository Dictionary of New Testament Words."

Bible Heart

Upon close examination one can ascertain and or determine the composition of the Bible heart. After all the scriptures are gathered and studied that mention the heart, one may deduce that "the heart consists of the intellect or thinking ability; emotions; the will or volition; and the conscience. Jesus mentioned "understanding with their heart" (John 12: 40). Hence, "the intellect or reasoning ability resides in the Bible heart." The Bible speaks of the heart "possessing emotion (John 14: 1). Emotions such as joy, love, and desire are emotions said to emanate from the heart (John 16: 22; Matthew 22: 37; 5: 28)." The expression "willing heart" is a reference to the will of man being located in his heart (Exodus 35: 5). The language "pricked in their heart" is an allusion to "the conscience or that part of the heart that pains us when we do wrong (Acts 2:37)." This, then, is the Bible heart. Sometimes a particular scripture that mentions "heart" may have the emotions or will in mind; sometimes the intellect or conscience may be the main thought. Having established of what the Bible heart consists, let us now examine some relevant facts about the heart.

Before we note some of the most common diseases of the Bible heart (heart of man), let's look at the condition of a pure heart:

- In Genesis God made man in His own image.
- Man was perfect, his heart was pure and clean.
- Man had a right relationship with God.
- God would come down in the cool of the day and talk with man.

- Yes, man's heart, his intellect/thinking ability, emotions, will or volition, and conscience knew no guile.
- Man received the authority to dominate the fish of the sea and everything upon the earth, including the animals and birds (Genesis 1:26–30).
- Adam and his wife Eve had it all.

Enter the serpent

Eve was tempted and her heart failed—she lusted with her eyes after the forbidden fruit and as the story goes, Adam became a willing victim to the tempter's snare, and they both fell spiritually (read the story in Genesis the third chapter). Their hearts were no longer pure, the once magnificent intellect would eventually be wasted in toiling and sweating; miserably eking out a mere existence instead of enjoying the superior lifestyle God had created them to live.

The price paid for the disease called sin (heart failure):

- Adam and Eve have now claimed the dubious distinction of becoming the first sinners in the history of creation.
- Man's heart has been tarnished beyond recognition, and every man woman and child must carry this heavy burden called sin, the price for having fallen short of the glory of God (Romans 3:23).
- The heart is messed up. Jeremiah 17:9 (NIV) says that "the heart is deceitful above all things and beyond cure. Who can know it?"
- Another translation (ESV) states "The heart is deceitful above all things, and desperately sick; who can understand it?
- But here is a translation (GW) that actually addresses the heart in terms of its reference to the mind, "The

human mind is the most deceitful of all things. It is incurable. No one can understand how deceitful it is."

This takes us to the actual text and the circumstances surrounding such a plea. David, "a man after God's own heart" soon discovered that his heart needed a transplant. The man of God, according to the scripture, had not only lusted after another man's wife but committed adultery with the woman; impregnated her, and had her husband killed in an effort to cover up his dastardly deeds. What a wicked, deceitful heart!

Therefore, Psalm 51 was written as contrition, to appease our gracious and loving God, who is also a God of judgment. So, in Psalm 51:10, David writes: "Create in me a clean heart." Adam Clarke's Commentary on Psalm 51 suggests that when David wrote this verse he was saying in essence "Mending will not avail; my heart is altogether corrupted; it must be new made, made as it was in the beginning" (and I would add that at one time David's heart must have been pure because the Bible said that God referred to him as a man after His own heart (Acts 13:22).

So, what happened to David's heart? We don't have to look very far to recognize the dilemma that was David's because it's the same dilemma we have found ourselves in right now. Sin has made our hearts deceitful and desperately wicked. We need a cure; and like David we must ask for a new heart. There are no known cures, according to Jeremiah 17:9. Therefore a replacement of the old heart is vital if we are to avoid certain spiritual death. Jesus said in Matthew 13:15, "For this people's heart has become calloused; they hardly hear with their ears, and they have closed their eyes. Otherwise they might see with their eyes, hear with their ears, understand with their hearts and be converted, and I would heal them."

What is your heart disease?

Romans 1:21 states, "Because that, when they knew God, they glorified him not as God, neither were thankful; but became vain in their imaginations, and their foolish heart was darkened." In addition, verses 28–32 provide a survey of the human condition as a result of a diseased heart:

> And even as they did not like to retain God in their knowledge, God gave them over to a reprobate mind, to do those things which are not convenient; Being filled with all unrighteousness, fornication, wickedness, covetousness, maliciousness; full of envy, murder, debate, deceit, malignity; whisperers, backbiters, haters of God, despiteful, proud, boasters, inventors of evil things, disobedient to parents, without understanding, covenant-breakers, without natural affection, implacable, unmerciful: who knowing the judgment of God, that they which commit such things are worthy of death, not only do the same, but have pleasure in them that do them.

Romans 6:23 provides a silver lining when it states, "For the wages of sin is death; but the gift of God is eternal life through Jesus Christ." God has given man a way out of his condition. The Apostle Paul states in Romans 5:8 that "God commendeth his love toward us, in that, while we were yet sinners, Christ died for us." Glory to God! John 3:16 tells us that "God so loved the world that he gave his only begotten son that whosoever believes on him will not perish but have eternal life." That's enough to make me want to stop and shout "Hallelujah."

Unlike the physical heart, the Bible heart (heart of man) must be replaced with a heart that loves God and his fellow humans. Mark 12:30–31 commands us to:

Love the Lord thy God with all thy heart, and with all thy soul, and with thy mind, and with all thy strength: this is the first commandment. And the second is like, namely this, "Though shalt love thy neighbour as thyself. There is none other commandment greater than these.

Understanding the critical condition of man's heart, God spoke through the Prophet Jeremiah, saying in chapter 29:13, "And ye shall seek me, and find me, when ye shall search for me with all your heart." Are you seeking God or are you wrapped up in the things of this world, side-tracked, preoccupied with things that will cause further damage to your heart? Lay aside your heavy burdens and turn your heart toward your maker. In Matthew 11:29 Jesus makes an offer you would be wise not to refuse, offering relief from the pressures that threaten to shatter your heart: "Take my yoke upon you and learn from me, for I am gentle and humble in heart, and you will find rest for your souls."

Accept the Great Physician's prescription—it will cost you nothing. Christ's death on the cross entitles "whosoever" (that's you and me) the opportunity to be reconciled with God "For he hath made him to be sin for us, who knew no sin; that we might be made the righteousness of God" (2 Corinthians 5:21). Allow the healing Spirit of the living God transform your heart and make you whole again.

The actual heart transplant begins when we "confess with our mouth the Lord Jesus, and believe in our heart that God raised him from the dead, and we are saved (Romans 10:9). But here is the kicker in the next verse, "For with the heart man believeth unto righteousness, and with the mouth confession is made unto salvation." Then, in 2 Corinthians 5:17 the word of God declares, "Therefore if any man be in Christ, he is a new creature: old things are passed away; behold all things are become new."

Becoming a new creation is to embark on a journey to develop the mind of Christ and emulate the humility that characterizes our Lord. Philippians 2:5–7 reads, "Let this mind be in you, which was also in Christ Jesus: who being in the form of God thought it not robbery to be equal with God: But made himself of no reputation and took upon him the form of a servant, and was made in the likeness of men." The new heart must be protected and nourished.

- Proverbs 4:23 suggests, "Above all else, guard your heart, for it is the wellspring of life
- Whatever you allow inside of you will either give life or destroy it.
- Proverbs 14:30 states that "A heart at peace gives life to the body, but envy rots the bones."
- Proverbs 17:22, "A cheerful heart is good medicine, but a crushed spirit dries up the bones."
- Psalm 1:1–3 "Blessed is the man who does not walk in the counsel of the wicked or stand in the way of sinners or sit in the seat of mockers. But his delight is in the law of the LORD, and on his law he meditates day and night. He is like a tree planted by streams of water, which yields its fruit in season and whose leaf does not wither. Whatever he does prospers."
- 1 John 1:9, "If we confess our sins he is faithful and just to forgive us our sins and to cleanse us from all unrighteousness."

That's it in a nutshell folks, the physical heart and the Bible heart (intellect or thinking ability; emotions; the will or volition; and the conscience) can be infected by diseases. While the cures for the physical heart require human intervention in the form of medical science, the Bible heart needs to be reconciled with its Creator. Both hearts need protection and nourishment. The former, depends on proper diet, exercise, rest, et cetera, and the Bible heart requires the blood of Jesus, the word of God, prayer, laughter, and godliness with contentment. People of God, it's a matter of the heart.

Pray with me: "Create in me a clean heart, O God and renew a right spirit within me." Like your servant David I pray according to Psalm 119:11, "Thy word have I hid in mine heart, that I might not sin against thee." Help me, Father God to guard my heart, in Jesus' name. Amen.

What's the one thing you desire most?

"The one thing I ask of the Lord—the thing I seek most—is to live in the house of the Lord all the days of my life, delighting in the Lord's perfections and meditating in his Temple" (Psalm 27:4, NLT)

If you had to choose one thing in this life, what would it be? Would you ask for riches, fame, personal success, the best wife or husband and a lifetime of happiness together? What would be your heart's desire—that one thing that would bring you bliss? The Psalmist David, according to our text, desired just one thing. He wanted more than anything else to spend time with God and to delight in His presence. Could it be that David knew something many of us today don't or have failed to comprehend? The answer is a resounding yes.

David understood that seeking first the kingdom of God, which was later taught by Jesus in Matthew 6:33 would open the door to divine prosperity. Psalm 37:4 instructs believers to "Take delight in the Lord, and he will give you your heart's desires." David knew that that one desire—the desire to put God first, to delight in Him would lead to other desires being addressed by his Provider. The Man of God was quite aware that "... they that seek the LORD shall not want any good *thing*" (Psalm 34:10). Friend, David's example should motivate us to shift our primary focus from the desire for "stuff" to developing a thirst for God and the things of God.

Cut them loose (put them out)

When they came to the home of the synagogue leader, Jesus saw the commotion and the weeping and wailing. He went inside and spoke to the people. "Why all this weeping and commotion?" he asked. "The child isn't dead; she is only asleep." The crowd laughed at him, but he told them all to go outside. Then he took the little child's father and mother and his three disciples into the room where the girl was lying. Holding her hand, he said to her, "Get up, little girl!" (Mark 5:38–41 NLT)

The story of Jairus and his daughter provides many lessons for the believer but today, let's focus on the importance of having the right people around us in the most crucial hour of need. If your so-called friends, church sisters/brothers, family members, and others can't believe God with you for your miracle, it's time to put them out, severing ties. Doubt and unbelief have no place in the hall of faith.

There are some who will weep and mourn over your circumstance, thinking that God is through with you; that your case is hopeless, and your comeback is anything but possible. Some will even mock when you tell them that God is not through with you yet. They will ask "Can your dry bones, your seemingly dead situation, prospect, ministry, career, marriage, or wanton child live again?" Child of God, though some have given up on you and have already arranged the burial, the Lord is saying this is not the end; it's revival time. Your miracle is about to happen. The thing you have believed God for will become a reality when you have cut them loose and the room of doubt and unbelief has become a hall of faith.

From knowledge to understanding

"The fear of the Lord is the beginning of wisdom: and the knowledge of the Holy One results in understanding" (Proverbs 9:10).

Knowledge is defined in Webster's College Dictionary as acquaintance with facts, truths, or principles; general erudition. Understanding, on the other hand, is defined in the same source as comprehension. It follows then that one may know the facts about a thing, situation, or God and not have an understanding of those facts. There has to be some form of processing of the facts in order to get to a level of understanding. The text is saying that it's not enough to know the facts about God's word; one must have a personal relationship with the author and finisher of our faith in order to reach an understanding of who He is. The process takes time and is dependent on the type and level of relationship we choose to pursue.

Ask any married couple about their relationship and invariably you will hear a recurring theme in the discussion: knowing a person and living with them are two different things. One really doesn't get to understand the true nature of a person unless or until one spends time perusing the idiosyncrasies, likes, dislikes, habits, and the true nature of that person. How many times do we hear someone declare "I thought I knew him or her?" Discovering the other side of a mate could have a positive or negative impact on the relationship.

Often, we become engaged and eventually "tie the knot" with people based on preconceived notions or invalid assumptions of who we think they are. Is it little wonder then that over half of all marriages dissolve, leaving many folks with broken dreams, disappointments, and heartache? Percy Sledge, a Rhythm and Blues singer of the 1950s and '60s warned in one of his hit songs: "Take time to know her—love is not an overnight thing." It's important that a couple look with searching hearts beneath the façade of the initial infatuation stage and spend quality time learning about the other person to get to a deeper level of knowledge and understanding about each other.

The good news is that our relationship with God, though it begins with knowledge, does get deeper, more intriguing, and sweeter over time, as long as we commit/surrender to Him; and let His word sanctify us. Our Lord desires that we know Him, become intimate with Him, and reach a more profound level of understanding in Him. Adam and Eve were created in the image of God for the expressed purpose of worshipping and experiencing intimate fellowship with their Creator (Genesis 1–2). The relationship lost its intimacy and trust when Adam and Eve failed to live according to God's word to them.

Conversely, in Genesis 5:24 we read of a man named Enoch who "walked with God: and he was not; for God took him." To walk with God is to spend time getting to know, obey, and conform to His way. Jesus said in Matthew 11:29, "Take my yoke upon you, and learn of me; for I am meek and lowly in heart: and ye shall find rest unto your souls." The Apostle Paul declares in Philippians 3:10, "That I may know him, and the power of his resurrection, and the fellowship of his sufferings, being made conformable unto his death."

Friend, giving one's heart to the Lord is the beginning of a relationship, in which the more intimate we become with Him, the more of Himself He reveals to us. Over time, we will develop the mind of Christ and exhibit characteristics and attributes unique to his image. Second Corinthians 3:18 states "But we all, with open face beholding as in a glass (mirror) the glory of the Lord, are changed into the same image from glory to glory, even as by the Spirit of the Lord."

Let your light shine brightly; love one another

Friends, only when we walk as Jesus walked are we able to reflect the True Light of love.

Those who say they live in God should live their lives as Jesus did. If any one says, "I am living in the light," but hates a Christian brother or sister, that person is still living in darkness. Anyone who loves other Christians is living in the light and does not cause anyone to stumble. Anyone who hates a Christian brother or sister is living and walking in darkness. Such person is lost, having been blinded by darkness." Put the hurts and differences aside; forgive and let the light of love shine brightly today (1 John 2:6, 9–11).

Speak to your Goliath today!

Then said David to the Philistine, Thou comest to me with a sword, and with a spear, and with a shield: but I come in the name of the Lord of hosts, the God of the armies of Israel, whom thou hast defied. This day will the Lord deliver thee into mine hand; and I will smite thee, and take thine head from thee; and I will give the carcasses of the host of the Philistines this day unto the fowls of the air, and to the wild beasts of the earth, that all the earth may know that there is a God in Israel. And all this assembly shall know that the Lord saveth not with sword and spear: for the battle is the Lord's, and he will give you into our hands" (1 Samuel 17:45–47)

Child of God, don't look at the enemy's size, ferocity, influence, power, or the odds against you, for "greater is he that is in you, than he that is in the world." Speak to your circumstance today; remind the challenger of the awesome power of your God. Like David in the text, tell the ungodly giant in your life that your salvation is sure and his destruction has been predetermined. Warn him that "The weapons of our warfare are not carnal but mighty through God to the pulling down of strongholds" (2 Corinthians 10:4).

Declare to the spiritual bully that our God is the Great Deliverer. Boast on the Lord God of Israel, for He has never lost a battle; and He is dressed in His omnipotence, ready to fight on our behalf right now. We have been promised all the support we would ever need, to enter any fray, face any situation, with absolute confidence. Joshua 1:9 states, "Have not I commanded thee? Be strong and of a good courage; be not afraid, neither be thou dismayed: for the Lord thy God is with thee withersoever thou goest." He doesn't stand a chance against the elect of God.

Friend, the Apostle Paul exhorts us to "Be strong in the Lord, and in the power of His might" (Ephesians 6:10). Stand firm, shout loudly in anticipation of certain victory. The one who orchestrated the terror against us, the accuser of the brethren has been overpowered. Speak to your Goliath today!

Have you received the promised Comforter/Counselor?

> But I tell you the truth: It is for your good that I am going away. Unless I go away, the Counselor will not come to you; but if I go, I will send him to you. When he comes, he will convict the world of guilt in regard to sin and righteousness and judgment: in regard to sin, because men do not believe in me; in regard to righteousness, because I am going to the Father, where you can see me no longer; and in regard to judgment, because the prince of this world now stands condemned. "I have much more to say to you, more than you can now bear. But when he, the Spirit

of truth, comes, he will guide you into all truth. He will not speak on his own; he will speak only what he hears, and he will tell you what is yet to come. He will bring glory to me by taking from what is mine and making it known to you. All that belongs to the Father is mine. That is why I said the Spirit will take from what is mine and make it known to you. (John 16:7–14, NIV).

Friend, please allow the word of God to minister to your heart today (without my comments); and if you have not yet received the Comforter/Counselor who guides us into all truth, ask the Lord earnestly and you will receive this gift.

Do your words give life?

Proverbs 18:21 states, "Death and life are in the power of the tongue: and they that love it shall eat the fruit thereof."

Many Christians are unaware that the words they speak could have either a negative or positive impact on their children, spouses, marriages, and determine success or failure in life. The text advises that we have the option of speaking death-causing or life-giving words. Consequently, we are to be careful of what we say and how we say it because we generally reap whatever we have sown.

Parents make negative deposits into their children's lives without realizing the lasting effect. They say things like: "why can't you be like ... (usually someone they deem more progressive or better behaved); you are just like your father—he was no good and you are no good; you are a good-for-nothing boy/girl." Should we be surprised when our boys and girls grow up to be troubled adults, exhibiting self-destructive and antisocial behavior? We need to understand that "Negative words can have lasting, harmful and unintended effects on children" according to Deborah Wood, PhD, Child Development

Specialist. But a similar problem exists in our adult-to-adult relationships and causes just as much damage to the psyche.

In our adult relationships, some husbands and wives seem to have a penchant for belittling, "cutting down" their spouses, not knowing that little by little they are inflicting deep emotional and psychological trauma on individuals they had promised to love, cherish, and honor. There are reported cases where spouses were berated and told that no other man or woman would ever want to be with them. How tragic! Of course, we could fill a library with examples of situations in which the tongue was deployed in ways that were detrimental to the well-being and prosperity of others and self. But we shall not end on such a morbid note. There is a better way, a way that brings life and blessing.

Friends, with the love of the Lord in our hearts and the wisdom of God as our guide, let us embark upon a purposeful effort to speak life and blessing over ourselves and each other. Words are life-giving or death producing. Proverbs 18:20 declares, "A man's belly shall be satisfied with the fruit of his mouth; and with the increase of his lips shall he be filled." Do we want to raise healthy, productive children, enjoy deep, loving, lasting relationships with our spouses, and live in true prosperity? The answer is quite simple: we must learn to speak only words that bring edification to the hearer, even if the only one listening is the speaker. Let us speak life!

A scriptural, godly perspective

Are we justified in praying for the destruction of our enemies? Some time ago, I read a post on one of the social network sites in which an individual prayed with passion for the destruction of his enemies. Immediately, the Spirit of the Lord reminded me of the Sermon on the Mount where in Matthew 5:43–48, Jesus taught the opposite:

You have heard that it was said, "Love your neighbor and hate your enemy." But I tell you, love your enemies and pray for those who persecute you, that you may be children of your Father in heaven. He causes his sun to rise on the evil and the good, and sends rain on the righteous and the unrighteous. If you love those who love you, what reward will you get? Are not even the tax collectors doing that? And if you greet only your own people, what are you doing more than others? Do not even pagans do that? Be perfect, therefore, as your heavenly Father is perfect.

What? "Love your enemies and pray for those who persecute you?" The word of God says in Isaiah 55:8, "For my thoughts *are* not your thoughts, neither *are* your ways my ways, saith the Lord." Therefore, our approach or response to any situation, no matter how frustrating, should be from a scriptural, godly perspective.

Your enemy is afraid; it's time to reclaim your stuff.

Genesis 20:8, "Therefore Abimelech rose early in the morning, and called all his servants, and told all these things in their ears: and the men were sore afraid."

What were "these things" that Abimelech told his servants? Briefly, Abraham went into Gerar which was ruled by King Abimelech. The man of God was afraid to admit that the beautiful woman with him, Sarah was his wife. Abraham thought that the strong man, Abimelech, would kill him and take Sarah. So, out of fear he told the people of Gerar that Sarah was his sister. Like Job, the thing that Abraham feared most would come upon him.

As anticipated, Abimelech sent and took Sarah but would not be able to touch her. God had intervened on Abraham's behalf, and Abimelech received a strong warning in a dream one night. The Lord told Abimelech that the consequence of his action would be certain death, unless he returned Sarah to her husband. Now it was Abimelech's turn to experience real fear. As a result, verse 14 of Genesis 20 states, "And Abimelech took sheep, and oxen, and menservants, and women servants, and gave them unto Abraham, and restored him Sarah his wife." The God who had promised to bless Abraham and his seed had shown up in His dreadfulness.

Child of God, I decree and declare, in the name of Jesus Christ of Nazareth and the authority of the word of God that whatever or whomever made you afraid will be made to fear our great and awesome God. That the one who stole your position on the job will have to give it up. Those who have been blocking your progress to the next level will flee, when no one is chasing them. Your prodigal sons and daughters, the wayward husband or wife will refocus and come home. Yes, all the good things that the enemy has stolen shall be restored, according to the word of God.

Tell your enemy "It's all good."

Genesis 50:20 (NLT), "As far as I am concerned, God turned into good what you meant for evil."

You may not know the "why" behind your struggles at this moment in time, but trust God anyway. Often, God orchestrates happenings in our lives in ways that baffle the finite mind. For example, Joseph dreamt of future prosperity and superiority (Genesis 37). Instead, he experienced unimaginable hardships for almost fourteen years following, as his dreams took him through a circuitous path of hatred, involuntary servitude, false accusation, and imprisonment (Genesis 39).

Through it all, Joseph kept the faith. He remained honorable before his God, even in the dungeon of forgetfulness. Child of God, keep your focus; God is not through with you yet. Keep the dream alive because your gift is about to make room for you. Your future is still tied up in a dream. Your prison is separated from the palace by only a dream and very soon your future of prosperity and superiority will be manifested (Genesis 40–41).

Soon your purpose will be made clear, and those that planned your demise will kneel before you in fear, expecting your revenge. However, like Joseph in Genesis 50:19–20, you will say to them "Don't be afraid of me. Am I God, to judge and punish you? As far as I am concerned, God turned into good what you meant for evil. He brought me to a high position today so I could save the lives of many people." Friend, tell your enemy, "It's all good."

Chapter Three

GOD LOVES SINNERS (DO YOU?)

"For God so loved the world that He gave his only begotten son that whosoever believeth in him should not perish but have everlasting life" (John 3:16).

Do we loathe sin or sinners?

    Whether we like it or not, this is a valid question and a very relevant one at that. I will not and cannot point at anyone but me. I'm as guilty as any other, from the standpoint of being self-righteous and indifferent toward those the church deems incorrigible and doomed to perish. Sinners, some say, deserve what's coming to them, even as we hurl sermons at them, laced with hell, fire, and brimstone. They have no excuse. The word does warn in Proverbs 13:15 that "Good understanding gives favor: but the way of the transgressor is hard." We love that verse, especially when we see someone, "not living right" or overtly toying with sin.

    Then there is Romans 6:23: "For the wages of sin is death but the gift of God is eternal life in Christ Jesus our Lord."

Many of us tend to become fixated on the wages of sin, which does scare some folks into the faith; however, the sad truth is that we hardly emphasize the goodness of God exhibited in the option of an eternal life with the King of Kings. How many times, in a fit of righteous anger, we verbally castigate and condemn someone to his or her just punishment in "hell" because we believed that their behavior was so egregious as to warrant swift and harsh punishment.

Our concept of Father God

Often, our concept of God the Father is shaped by our experiences with our earthly fathers or experiences as a result of not having or knowing a daddy. Therefore, if one grew up in a loving, caring home with a responsible and loving father, one generally derives a good concept of a father figure from that relationship. On the other hand, if one's experiences precluded the presence of a father figure, or included a relationship with a father, based on emotional and physical abuse, one would have some difficulty understanding the loving kindness of Father God and would perhaps view Him as a punisher. Of course, there are exceptions to every rule.

How do you view Father God? Is He your Daddy or your Punisher? The Bible teaches that God is loving but just. Try, if you will, to think of a good father in the home. He scolds and perhaps uses the rod of correction a few times, but not in a manner that will bring terror or fear to the child. A good father shows love even when he corrects his children. The Bible says that "For whom the Lord loveth he chasteneth, and scourgeth every son whom he receiveth." God loves us, and if we get out of line he will reprimand in a way that will get us back on the right track—if we are not rebellious.

Personal Story: From a message of damnation to love

About a year ago, after signing on to a social network site, my first order of business after linking up with new friends and almost-forgotten acquaintances, was to take a stance for Jesus. Of course, I commenced to present a gospel showcasing my love for the Lord and damnation for sinners; forgetting that according to Romans 3:23, "All have sinned and come short of the glory of God." This continued for several months until the Lord caused me to cross paths with a pastor from Africa, who will remain anonymous at this time.

This man of God read my posts for a while and would, in his subtle way, pour a simple message of God's grace and mercy, God's unmatchable love for all of us humans, into my spirit. I must admit that after much resistance, the Lord softened my heart and changed my focus from God the Punisher to a loving, caring God. The God who loved us so much that "He sent His only begotten son that whosoever believeth in Him should not perish but have everlasting life" (John 3:16). I suggest to you that this paradigm shift was difficult because I could still see in the back of my mind—father punisher.

Honestly, the process took some time, and after much back and forth that included the severance of communication with the man of God, a few sneak previews of his posts, and finally, a chance meeting with a passage of scripture found in the book of Romans 2:4 (NLT) "Don't you see how wonderfully kind, tolerant, and patient God is with you? Does this mean anything to you? Can't you see that his kindness is intended to turn you from your sin?" The King James Version puts the verse this way "Or despisest thou the riches of his goodness and forbearance and longsuffering; not knowing that the goodness of God leadeth thee to repentance?" Hallelujah!

Do you have a testimony of the goodness of God? Is there a praise report that brings tears of joy and gladness when you think or speak about it? The problem that only God could have solved, the one you promised God that if He got you out unscathed, you would serve Him for the rest of your life. Remember? Or that health scare that caused you to seek God with all your heart, and He showed up with healing in His wings and did what no physician could have done? What about the marriage that was careening out of control until God stepped in and saved the family from despair. If the truth is told, many of us were drawn to God by His goodness and love for us.

It's not God's intention to punish

Child of God, the Lord had no intention of being a punisher, when He said in Genesis 1:26 "Let us make human beings in our image, to be like us. They will reign over the fish in the sea, the birds in the sky, the livestock, all the wild animals on the earth, and the small animals that scurry along the ground." God loved us. He wanted man to be in His image to rule and reign over every living thing upon the face of this earth and in the sea. God wanted a partner and a companion on the earth with whom He could fellowship and have discourse in the cool of the day.

Our heavenly Father desired to be in constant communion with man; He wanted someone to whom He would reveal His secrets of leadership and godly governance, someone who would walk in His way. But man strayed. Yes, sin brought about a spiritual separation between man and God. Thus, man's disobedience led to his relegation to a life of hard labor, stripped of his original spiritual and intellectual prowess.

As time went by, man's wickedness grew to heights unparalleled since the creation, and God decided to destroy the earth. But the Bible said that Noah found grace in the eyes of the Lord. Noah and his family were the only righteous people on the face of the earth at that time. Noah epitomized the Psalm chapter 1 believer. He walked with God; therefore, when God decided to destroy wickedness from the face of the earth, "Noah found grace in the eyes of the Lord" and his family was spared. O the love and mercy of God!

It was not God's will to destroy mankind and had they repented during Noah's 120 years of preaching, they would have been spared (Genesis 6). The Bible reads in 2 Peter 3:9 "The Lord is not slack concerning his promise, as some men count slackness; but is long suffering to us-ward, not willing that any should perish, but that all should come to repentance." If that's not love, I don't know what is.

God truly loves the sinner. Jeremiah 3:14 says "Return, O backsliding children, says the Lord; for I am married to you. I will take you, one from a city and two from a family and I will bring you to Zion." Friend, we usually marry the one we love. Church, Jesus wants every sinner to be a part of the body of Christ, to be His bride. That's a true love story, indeed. Hear what Hosea 2:16 has to say about the matter, "And it shall be in that day, says the Lord, that you will call me husband; and no longer call me my master." God loves his children in a very intimate way. His desire is to have every wanderer, every unstable ingrate to come close enough, to enter into the bride-chamber with Him.

Isaiah 53:6 declares "All we like sheep have gone astray; we have turned every one to his own way; and the Lord hath laid on him the iniquity of us all." Come to Jesus, the lamb who takes away the sin of the world, God's only begotten son. He died for you and me. Romans 5:8 states, "But God commendeth his love toward us, in that, while we were yet sinners, Christ died for us.

Do you love the sinner?

Jesus told a parable of a young man, popularly referred to as the prodigal son, to emphasize the tremendous love a Father has for his child. In essence, the story depicts God's unyielding love for the sinner or backslider. For our purposes here we'll pick up the story in: Luke 15:18–19, "I will arise and go to my father, and will say unto him, Father, I have sinned against heaven, and before thee, and am no more worthy to be called thy son: make me as one of thy hired servants." I'll take the liberty here to interject a story of someone I knew, a boy with a promising future who left the church and his father's house and joined up with members of a notorious street gang.

After many years in a life shrouded in smoke, violence, faded dreams, and missed opportunities, the young man awoke from his slumber, dusted off the slop, and returned home. As the tale unfolds, we see a penitent son in the trembling, thankful arms of a gracious, loving father. One would think that the entire household would have erupted in a concerted, ecstatic outburst of thunderous cheers but amidst the tumult there was protest. The older son, the good child, took offense to the merriment and could not appreciate, in his unforgiving heart, the fact that daddy would weep with joyous exuberance over his prodigal brother.

How could father ignore the good sibling's years of loyalty and unfailing servitude and be so enamored with a delinquent? Where is the fairness in all of this display of his father's undying, unreserved affection toward the returning miscreant child? (Luke 15:25–30). Who could be upset with and heap blame upon this doting, gentle father after so many years of sleepless nights, stockpiling grace upon grace in anticipation of the return of a once lost and troubled son?

Some church folk get upset and annoyed when the notorious or obvious sinner escapes his "just punishment" and is saved. Some have not understood the mercy and grace of Abba Father. Why should some low-down menace to society be received with loving, outstretched arms and given the right hand of fellowship? The answer, though complex in the natural, excites much simplicity in the spiritual. Our father God said in Jeremiah 3:14 that He is married to the backslider, and Jesus said in Matthew 9:13, "I am not come to call the righteous but sinners to repentance." Hallelujah!

In Luke 15:31–32 Jesus explains the father's reasoning, as he hoped to pacify the disgruntled son, "Son, thou art ever with me, and all that I have is thine. It was meet (fitting) that we should make merry, and be glad: for this thy brother was dead, and is alive again; and was lost, and is found." The people of God should celebrate when a sinner has been reconciled with his heavenly Father.

Friend, do you love the sinner enough to welcome him unconditionally into the kingdom? Or, are you secretly harboring some degree of resentment toward the unsaved, wishing that God would judge them? One does not have to go very far to hear the fire and brimstone messages being flung at sinners, and they do have a place and serve an important purpose in the preaching of the word of God. But that should not become a substitute for the gospel of Jesus Christ. Gospel means good news. The good news is "For God so loved the world, that he gave his only begotten son, that whosoever believeth in him should not perish, but have everlasting life." The good news is all about God's unconditional love for humanity.

Let me end with a story entitled "How a Young Irishman Opened Moody's Eyes" told by D. L. Moody, the famous preacher who founded Moody Bible Institute in Chicago:

> I want to tell you how I got my eyes open to the truth that God loves the sinner. When I went over to Europe I was preaching in Dublin, when a young fellow came up to the platform and said to me that he wanted to come to America and preach. He had a boyish appearance; did not seem to be over seventeen years old. I measured him all over, and he repeated his request, and asked me when I was going back. I told him I didn't know; probably I should not have told

him if I had known. I thought he was too young and inexperienced to be able to preach. In course of time I sailed for America, and hadn't been here long before I got a letter from him, dated New York, saying that he had arrived there. I wrote him a note and thought I would hear no more about him, but soon I got another letter from him, saying that he was coming soon to Chicago, and would like to preach. I sent him another letter, telling him if he came to call upon me, and closed with a few common-place remarks. I thought that would settle him, and I would hear no more from him. But in a very few days after he made his appearance. I didn't know what to do with him. I was just going off to Iowa, and I went to a friend and said: "I have got a young Irishman—I thought he was an Irishman, because I met him in Ireland—and he wants to preach. Let him preach at the meetings—try him, and if he fails, I will take him off your hands when I come home." When I got home—I remember it was on Saturday morning—I said to my wife: "Did that young man preach at the meetings?" "Yes." "How did they like him?" "They liked him very much," she replied: "He preaches a little different from you; he preaches that God loves sinners." I had been preaching that God hated sinners; that he had been standing behind the sinners with a double-bladed sword, ready to cut the heads of the sinners off. So I concluded if he preached different from me, I would not like him. My prejudice was up. Well, I went down to the meeting that night, and saw them coming in with their Bibles with them. I thought it was curious. It was something strange to see the people coming in with Bibles, and listen to the flutter of the leaves. The young man gave out his text, saying: "Let us turn to the third chapter of John, and sixteenth verse: 'For God so loved the world that He gave His only begotten Son that whosoever believeth in Him should not perish, but have everlasting life.'" He didn't divide up the text at all. He went from Genesis to Revelation, giving proof that God loved the sinner, and before he got through two or three of my sermons were spoiled. I have never preached them since. The following day—Sunday—there was an immense crowd flocking into the hall, and he said, "Let us turn to the third chapter of John, sixteenth verse: 'For God so loved the world that He gave His only begotten Son, that whosoever believeth in Him shall not perish, but have everlasting life;'" and he preached the fourth sermon from this verse. He just seemed to take the whole text and throw it at them, to prove that God loved the sinner, and that for six thousand years he had been trying to convince the world of this. I thought I had never heard a better sermon in my life. It seemed to be new revelation to all. Ah, I notice there are some of you here who remember those times; remember those nights. I got a new idea of the blessed Bible. On Monday night I went down and the young man said, "Turn to the third chapter of John, sixteenth verse;" and he seemed to preach better than ever. Proof after proof was quoted from Scripture to show how God loved us. I thought sure he had exhausted that text, but on Tuesday he took his Bible in his hand and said: "Turn to the third chapter of John, sixteenth verse, "and he preached the sixth sermon from that verse. He just seemed to climb over his subject, while he proved that there was nothing on earth like the love of Christ, and he said "If I can only convince men of His love, if I can but bring them to believe this text; the whole world will be saved." On Thursday he selected the same text, John 3:16, and at the conclusion of the sermon he said: "I have been trying to tell you for seven nights now, how Christ loves you, but I cannot do it. If I could borrow Jacob's ladder and climb up to heaven, and could see Gabriel there and ask him to tell me how much God loves me, he would only say, "God so loved the world that He gave His only begotten Son, that whosoever believeth in Him should not perish; but have everlasting life." How a man can go out of this tabernacle after hearing this text, saying, "God does not love me," is a mystery to me.

Let me give a bit of advice to anyone of us prone to beat folks over the head with fire and brimstone: It's easier to catch flies with honey than with vinegar. I believe that many more unsaved family members, children, husbands, wives, friends, and acquaintances would come to Jesus if they saw the love of God in us. Preach the truth but in love!

Pray with me: "Father God, thank you for loving us to the point of sending your only begotten son Jesus to die so that we might live the abundant life. May your word accomplish that which you have sent it out to do, in Jesus' mighty name! Amen.

Are you ready?

The Lord isn't really being slow about his promise to return, as some people think. No, he is being patient for your sake. He does not want anyone to perish, so he is giving more time for everyone to repent. 10) But the day of the Lord will come as unexpectedly as a thief. Then the heavens will pass away with a terrible noise, and everything in them will disappear in fire, and the earth and everything on it will be exposed to judgment (2 Peter 3:9–10, NLT).

God Loves Sinners (Do You?)

As much as we would like to think that this life is all that there is to living, we must be mindful of the promise Jesus made before He left this earth; that He would come again and receive us unto Himself (John 14:2–3). Every child of God ought to live each day, each hour, and each minute like a bride waiting for her bridegroom's imminent return. Let's adorn ourselves with holy garments of praise, punctuate the atmosphere with the sweet fragrance of prayer and moan in ecstatic anticipation, as we usher in the day of the Lord.

The text reminds us that the Lord is "patient for our sake" and that He delays His return to give folks time to repent. Jesus will return suddenly, without notice and only those who are ready will meet Him in His glorious splendor. Unfortunately for the unprepared, instead of joy there will be tears and judgment. Do you recall the parable our Lord told of the ten virgins who awaited the arrival of the bridegroom: five were wise and five foolish? The wise had bought enough oil for their lamps but the foolish virgins ran out of oil, went to purchase some at the eleventh hour and were locked out of the celebration. Jesus warns us to "Watch therefore, for ye know neither the day nor the hour wherein the Son of man cometh" (Matthew 25:1–30).

This message is not intended to cause fear but to lift us out of our earthbound, worldly stupor and elevate us into a state of sober reverence for God and the things of God. Hopefully, it will take us, like the songwriter said: to "a place of quiet rest, where sin cannot molest; near to the heart of God." Some of us have become far too distracted from the truth of God's word, parsing the word of God, putting in what's appealing to us, and eliminating that which convicts us. But the word says that Jesus, the Bridegroom, is coming back for His church, one without spot or blemish—and He's coming as a thief in the night. Are you ready?

Father, forgive them

Luke 23:34 says, "Then said Jesus, Father, forgive them; for they know not what they do."

Love compels us to forgive, in spite of their ingratitude, betrayal, the pain and the tears. Jesus recommended forgiveness for those who caused His innocent, sacrificial blood to flow freely from Calvary's cross "for they know not what they do." Child of God, those who have lied on you and caused you unbearable grief without reasonable cause need your forgiveness because they do not know what they are doing.

Saul did not know that he was in essence attacking the Lord with every stone he threw at members of the early Church (Acts 9:4). But Stephen, who was martyred under the direction and watchful eyes of Saul, like Jesus, knew that the purveyors of injustice did not know what they were doing, and he asked that they be forgiven (Acts 7:60). Saul became the Apostle Paul, who wrote most of the New Testament. You see my friend; God has a greater plan than the naked eyes can see.

The love of God reaches out to the sinner, even when he or she isn't aware of this all encompassing, ever-forgiving charity; its aim is to seek and to save the lost (Romans 5:8; Luke 19:10). So, we must forgive; when the crushing blows are falling and the knife is plunged into the back. We must forgive, as the answers elude us and the perpetrator doesn't know the real reason behind his or her actions. We must forgive, when the last word has been thrown and it ripped a deep wound in the bottom of the heart.

Yes, as difficult as it may seem, we must ask the Father to forgive them. No one said it would be easy, but love says "Father, forgive them; for they know not what they do." Friend, Jesus said "If I be lifted up, I will draw all men unto me" (John 12:32). Our love and willingness to forgive points the wicked to the cross, to Jesus who died that we all might be forgiven (John 3:16–17).

Have you been washed?

"Now Naaman captain of the host of the king of Syria, was a great man with his master, and honourable, because by him the Lord had given deliverance unto Syria; he was also a mighty man in valour, but he was a leper" (2 Kings 5:1).

Naaman was a man who had great power, status and wealth—everything a man could want—but his condition rendered him sick and vulnerable. He was a leper. In those days being afflicted with leprosy meant a life of shame, misfortune, and hopelessness. How is it possible for an individual to have all the trappings of respectability, notoriety, and success and at the same time be an outcast, a pariah?

Sadly, such contradiction is evident in the lives of some of us today. We hold high offices, wield extraordinary power, and command the respect of peers and superiors alike but are scarred by the scourge of sin. We preach great sermons and sing beautiful melodies of praise but are unclean and need to be washed in the blood of the Lamb. Anyone without Christ is like a leper, even with the symbols of success, and needs cleansing.

The man of God, in 2 Kings 5:10, advised Naaman to wash in Jordan seven times to receive his healing. Initially, he protested strongly and after a great deal of persuasion from a servant girl he obeyed and was healed (verses 11–14). Many folks have heard the message of the gospel of Jesus Christ preached over and over but are too proud to receive their cleansing. Friend, spiritual cleansing occurs only when one confesses that Jesus is Lord and believes in one's heart that God has raised Jesus from the dead (Romans 10:9). The scripture states that "Whosoever believeth on him shall not be ashamed" (Romans 10:11). Have you been washed?

Have you met the Lord?

Job 42:5 (KJV) "I have heard of thee by the hearing of the ear: but now mine eye seeth thee." The New Living Translation puts the text this way: "I have heard about you before, but now I have seen you with my own eyes."

Some of you may remember, as children singing this chorus: "At the cross at the cross where I first saw the light and the burden of my heart rolled away. It was there by faith I received my sight and now I am happy all the day." How many of us can say with all honesty that we saw the light, that we received sight? Think about it for a moment. Nicodemus had his born-again moment with Jesus; the Samaritan woman had her encounter at the well; Saul had his Damascus Road experience; and here we have Job with his eye-opening discovery of God. The question today is, have you met the Lord? Are your eyes open to the reality of who God is?

Our text brings us to a crescendo, if you will, of a long saga, filled with loss, grief, pain, and disillusionment endured by the righteous man, Job. The man of God defended his innocence while asking tough questions of God. Read the entire book of Job to get the scope of this man's tribulations and his ultimate encounter with God, played out between Job chapters 1 through 41. The word said that Job was righteous, the most righteous man of his day. But he had not, up to this point, met God for himself. Like most of us, Job had developed a concept of God based on what he had heard. Thank the Lord for men and women who propagate the gospel around the world and in our churches. Faith comes by hearing the word of God. But we need more than hearing and believing; we need revelation from a born-again perspective.

Job had heard his friends preaching and extolling the excellency of Almighty God. However, Job came face to face with the Great and Terrible One, by way of a whirlwind (Job 38–41). Have you come face to face with this awesome

God? The Lord desires to bring us into His Holy Place, to talk with us and instruct us on matters that pertain to life. So, in Job 42:5, he had what some would call his eureka moment, a revelation of the awesome majesty of God—the born-again enlightenment one acquires when human understanding fails and one is left trembling in humility and reverence before the throne of grace.

Job's eyes were opened, and at long last he could see through the eye of the Spirit, the King of Kings and Lord of Lords. Flesh had given place to faith in God and darkness acquiesced to light. Job had met the Lord. Perspectives change when we have met the Lord. We love more when we have met the Lord. Pride and vanity become relative bystanders as we travel by faith, in humility, with thanksgiving, singing amazing grace how sweet the sound that saved a wretch like me. I once was lost but now I'm found; was blind but now I see. Have you met the Lord? His name is Jesus. (See Job 1–42, John 3, Hebrews 11.)

Pray for our adversaries

It's scriptural to pray for those who have caused us grief, like Abraham did in Genesis 20:17, like Job did in chapter 42:10, and like Jesus did on the cross. Why? Because (1) the word of God states that vengeance belongs to God; (2) our blessing is tied to our obedience to the word of God; (3) God loves all humanity, even our enemies; and (4) it's not God's will that any should perish but that all should come to repentance. Now, let's pray for those who are causing us trouble: Father, forgive them for they do not know what they are doing. Speak to their hearts, Lord and bring them into a right relationship with you; in the name of Jesus.

God's love versus the Jonah syndrome

Luke 19:10 "For the Son of man came to seek and to save that which was lost."

If one believes that "those wicked people over there" ought to be punished for being disobedient to God and even relishes the thought of God meting out their total destruction without warning, one has the Jonah Syndrome. Just like the Prophet Jonah in the book of the Bible bearing his name, some folks today are disgusted with the idea that God is not willing that any person should perish but that all people should come to repentance (2 Peter 3:9). They believe that the wrath of God should be swift and definitive, leaving no room for repentance.

Have we forgotten that God's grace and mercy have been extended to all, even those evil people, "we good Christians" loathe with a passion? John 3:17 states "For God sent not his son into the world to condemn/judge the world; but that the world through him might be saved." Therefore, whether some of us like it or not, the commission is to go into the world and preach the good news, not to condemn or seek total annihilation of those "Ninevites."

The self-righteous, unlovely rhetoric that's being spewed at some of God's children by well-intentioned, modern day prophets goes contrary to the message of God's grace and hope for a sin-sick world. Friend, love reaches down to the sinner, the lost, the hopeless, and the undeserving and says "Come to me, all you that labor and are heavy laden, and I will give you rest" (Matthew 11:28). Are we filled with God's love for the unsaved or are we twenty-first-century Jonahs desiring their total destruction?

What must I do to be saved?

"Sirs, what must I do to be saved? And they said, Believe on the Lord Jesus Christ, and thou shalt be saved, and thy house" (Acts 16:30–31).

The text relates a familiar conversation between a jailer and Paul and Silas. As the story goes Paul and Silas were beaten and thrown in jail for disturbing the peace in Philippi (Acts 16:16–24). They sang and praised God during the night, and at midnight there was an earthquake during which they were freed supernaturally from their cell. The jailer, thinking that his prisoners had escaped, drew his sword and would have killed himself but was prevented by Paul (Acts 16:25–28). Having heard the prayer meeting and singing that took place earlier and being overwhelmed by the miracle that took place at midnight, the jailer asked a very profound question, "What must I do to be saved?" (Acts 16:30)

That question is as relevant today, perhaps more so than at any other time in the history of Christianity. A large number of people are claiming to be godly or spiritual, but fewer of them are voicing a belief in Jesus Christ (Isaiah 29:13). Anyone who watches some of the talk shows and music award shows on television has heard celebrities talk about their "God." But are all these people saved? Have they asked the question, "What must I do to be saved?" And if so, have they received an appropriate response?

Attending church, even getting emotional in church or speaking of God or the Holy Spirit on the world's stage is no guarantee that one is saved—that one has met and accepted Jesus Christ as Savior and Lord. Some people pay lip service to God but they neither know Him nor have they committed to being the righteousness of God through Jesus Christ (Matthew 15:8). Church, the people of the world are in a dark, confused state and need to experience, like the jailer, a midnight-like visit of the Holy One. This is possible if or when we begin to offer unto the Lord, true worship and praise that will induce a shaking of the very foundation of this world's system. Let the world witness a move of God, a revival that will bring them to their knees and compel them to ask, "What must I do to be saved?"

Like Paul and Silas, we must fill the earth (our churches, jails, television, and social media, etc.) with the only message that brings people to salvation, the gospel of Jesus Christ (Romans 10:9). Paul and Silas, according to Acts 16:31-32, said to the jailer "Believe on the Lord Jesus Christ, and thou shalt be saved, and thy house. And they spake unto him the word of the Lord, and to all that were in his house." We must go back to the original gospel of Jesus Christ because it is "the power of God unto salvation" and the only message that will turn on the light in the darkness of people's lives (Romans 1:16). That message will drive the congregant, entertainer, man, woman, boy, and girl to cry out, "What must I do to be saved?"

Chapter Four

WHO IS HE AND WHAT IS HE TO YOU?

> "And Jesus went out, and his disciples, into the towns of Caesarea Philippi: and by the way he asked his disciples, saying unto them, *who do men say that I am?* And they answered, John the Baptist: but some say, Elias; and others, one of the prophets. And he saith unto them, *But who say ye that I am?* And Peter answereth and saith unto him, Thou art the Christ. And he charged them that they should tell no man of him (Mark 8:27–30, italics mine)."

Who is He? (Who do men say that I am?) Are we able to investigate our way into knowledge of who He is in a manner similar to running a background check? What is He to you? (And who do you say that I am?) Have you had a revelation of who Jesus is; which has transformed your perception from merely head knowledge to a personal intimate relationship? Is there any specific thing that He has done for you that readily translates into a personal testimony of what Jesus means to you?

It's not uncommon for employers to do background checks on prospective employees. The résumé introduces the applicant to the employer or organization, outlining name, address, contact information; objective, work experience, accomplishments, and qualifications (Of course, résumés vary depending on the type of job or employment one is seeking). But, as we all know, people tend to embellish their résumé to suit the purpose. Therefore, it behooves the employer to do a thorough investigation into the credentials of each potential employee. The purpose of such a review is to ascertain whether the person is who he or she says he is—whether he or she prove to be an asset or a liability to the firm, company or business.

The intrusiveness of the background search will depend on the type of job, business, or profession for which one is applying. For example, to be hired as a medical doctor anywhere, one must have been properly educated and trained, licensed, Board Certified (if applicable), etc; and must withstand a review of past conduct (professionally and ethically). The same applies to all school board employees in the public school system. Prior to being hired or certified, each individual must submit to fingerprinting and rigorous FBI scrutiny of his or her past criminal record. The factory worker, nanny, banker, salesperson—everyone must withstand some kind of profile search, for lack of a better term, to determine his/her true identity.

Screening, you will agree with me, is necessary to rule out imposters, fakes, and phonies. I heard recently that experts are advising couples to do background investigations of their mate's personal history, including financial health, for overall suitability for marriage. Laugh if you will but one cannot be too cautious when dealing with the heart of man and its inclination to be wicked. Many innocent wives and husbands have been left heartbroken, victims of unscrupulous and financially irresponsible partners. Many a heartache could have been avoided if the proper vetting process had been undertaken.

One has to be sure in this day and age that one acquires adequate information on which to base the decision whether to pursue an intimate relationship with another person. Here we are, Saints, professing our faith in Jesus but do we really know who He is? Will a background check—launched in our own efforts lead us to the answer (the cookie cutter, one-size-fits-all answer)? Jesus asked His disciples, "Who do men say that I am?" He did not ask the question because He did not know who He was—Jesus asked the question to see if any among the throng that followed Him had received a revelation from the Spirit of God, as to His deity and more specifically, that He was their Messiah.

We know that this is so based on the followup question put to the disciples in verse 29, "But who say ye that I am?" Really, Jesus! You chose us, placed us under your tutelage, fed us; mesmerized us with miracles and parables, and now you are asking us to tell you who you are? The crowds that jostled for His wisdom, healings, and in a few cases, to be fed, thought that He was John the Baptist, Elijah, or some other prophet. There are some folks today who will say that Jesus was just a good rabbi, others will say that He is a prophet, and a large number will say that He was a great historical figure.

It's evident that other peoples' concept of Jesus will not adequately explain who He is to you. You must get this revelation for yourself. As much as we admire Billy Graham, the late E.V. Hill, and other great men and women of God, their revelation of who Jesus is will not suffice for you or me. Our aim should be like that of the Apostle Paul in Philippians 3:10, "That I may know him, and the power of his resurrection, and the fellowship of his sufferings, being made conformable unto his death." Child of God, we are faced with the question, who do you say that I am? Simon Peter, the rough and tumble, irritable, curse-you-in-a-minute disciple blurted out a response that Jesus acknowledged could only have come from the Holy Spirit. "You are the Christ," Peter exclaimed. Glory to God! Matthew 16:17 shows Jesus' response to Simon Peter, "And Jesus answered and said unto him, Blessed art thou, Simon Barjona: for flesh and blood hath not revealed *it* unto thee, but my Father which is in heaven."

Our personal investigation into the question of who Jesus is must begin with the Father. Let's take a look at what the word of God says about Jesus. We will not attempt to review every scripture verse that speaks to who Jesus is, but here are a few: Jesus said in John 10:30 "I and the Father are one" and in John 14:7 he said "If ye had known me, ye should have known my Father also: and from henceforth ye know him, and have seen him." Advancing his claim with much authority, when a disciple asked to see the Father, Jesus stated in John 14:9 "Have I been with you all this time, Philip, and yet you still don't know who I am? Anyone who has seen me has seen the Father! So why are you asking me to show him to you?"

Philip wanted more proof that this man who they had been calling master for several years was in fact God in the flesh. I take the liberty of interjecting here that if Jesus was our contemporary and had made those claims among this high tech generation, someone would have googled or performed some kind of a background search on Him. Can you imagine being on a boat during a storm and seeing this man rebuking the wind and the waves, as He did in Matthew 8? I'm sure our reaction would be similar to the disciples when they asked: "Who is this man? "Even the winds and waves obey him!" Who is He? What does God say about Him?

Matthew 3:17, "And a voice from heaven said, "This is my dearly loved Son, who brings me great joy." (Also Mark 1:11)

Psalm 2:17, "I will proclaim the decree of the LORD: He said to me, "You are my Son; today I have become your Father."

Who Is He And What Is He To You?

Isaiah 42:1, "Here is my servant, whom I uphold, my chosen one in whom I delight; I will put my Spirit on him and he will bring justice to the nations."

Mathew 12:18, "Here is my servant whom I have chosen, the one I love, in whom I delight; I will put my Spirit on him, and he will proclaim justice to the nations."

Matthew 17:5, "While he was still speaking, a bright cloud enveloped them, and a voice from the cloud said, 'This is my Son, whom I love; with him I am well pleased. Listen to him!'" (Also Mark 9:7)

Luke 9:35-36, "A voice came from the cloud, saying, "This is my Son, whom I have chosen; listen to him." When the voice had spoken, they found that Jesus was alone. The disciples kept this to themselves, and told no one at that time what they had seen."

2 Peter 1:17, "For he received from God the Father honour and glory, when there came such a voice to him from the excellent glory, this is my beloved Son, in whom I am well pleased."

The naysayer would perhaps ask the FBI and CIA to commence an exhaustive investigation into His qualifications. Will that help to explain who is He? Well, preliminary search has revealed that "In the beginning God" (Genesis 1:1). John 1:1 says, "In the beginning was the word and the word was with God, and the word was God." The evidence thus far points to a very powerful résumé. By now, even the very stoical investigator is shaking his head and could be heard mumbling a soft, barely audible "Praise the Lord." His once doubting fingers peruse the pages of this voluminous résumé and lingered for a while at John 14:6 "I am the way, the truth, and the life: no man comes unto the Father, but by me." Glory! He flipped back to John 1:29, "Behold the Lamb of God which taketh away the sin of the world" and then to Revelation 1:17, "Fear not; I am the first and last." With a softened heart and an open mind, the investigation continues into Jesus' work experience.

What about work experience?

Matthew 11:3 relates the story of the two disciples of John the Baptist who asked Jesus, Art thou he that should come, or do we look for another?" Jesus answered and said 'Go and show John again those things which ye do hear and see: The blind receive their sight, the lame walk, the lepers are cleansed, and the deaf hear, the dead are raised up, and the poor have the gospel preached to them.'

Who is He?

For unto us a child is born, unto us a son is given: and the government shall be upon his shoulder: and his name shall be called Wonderful, Counselor, The mighty God, The everlasting Father, The Prince of Peace. Of the increase of his government and peace there shall be no end, upon the throne of David, and upon his kingdom, to order it, and to establish it with judgment and with justice from henceforth even for ever. The zeal of the LORD of hosts will perform this" (Isaiah 9:6–7).

What is He to you?

Have you had an experience with this Jesus that will provide a satisfactory response to the inquisitor's question, what is he to you? To Simon Peter, He is the Christ. To the woman with the Alabaster box of ointment, Jesus was valuable and her gratefulness was reflected in her worship. She had sinned much but, praise the Lord, Jesus forgave her much. To the Samaritan woman at the well, Jesus was the spring of living waters. What is He to you? To Jairus, whose daughter Jesus raised from the dead, I'm sure He saw Jesus as the resurrection and the life. To blind Bartemeus, Jesus was the restorer of sight. What is He to you?

Jesus, name above every other name

Wherefore God also hath highly exalted him, and given him a name which is above every name. That at the name of Jesus every knee should bow, of things in heaven, and things in earth, and things under the earth; and that every tongue should confess that Jesus Christ is Lord, to the glory of God the Father" (Philippians 2:9–11).

Friend, if you don't know this Jesus, you have a choice to make. You may choose to bow now or bow later; confess Him now or confess Him later, but we all must bow and we all shall confess that Jesus is Lord. Remember, there can be no repentance after the grave, only judgment. Let's pray! Jesus, I accept you as my Savior and Lord; I believe in my heart that God raised you from the dead (Romans 10:9). Thank you, Lord Jesus for saving me. Now, find a church that teaches the full gospel, stay rooted and grounded in the word of God; and pray regularly, in the name of Jesus.

We worship you, Jesus!

It is unfortunate that in certain quarters of Christendom, some Hebrew language aficionados are waging strong opposition to the use of Jesus, as the official name of the Son of God. Scholarship notwithstanding, the question is why complicate the simple truth of the gospel with nonsensical debating. What a travesty! We are commissioned to preach the "Good News," in the only name, Greek, Hebrew, or English that has the power to save, heal, deliver, set free, and raise the dead. For centuries faithful followers have addressed Him by the name of Jesus and have seen His mighty hand at work, regardless of the translation used.

Maturity in the things of God negates any haggling over things that do not change the sinner into a saint, replace darkness with light, and deliver those who are bound (Hebrews 5:12–14). What is the point of being scholastically relevant but spiritually irrelevant? It makes no sense to have a form of godliness, a head knowledge of who Jesus is, but lack the power of His Spirit (2 Timothy 3:5). It's time to change lives in the name of Jesus, the name above every other name, that at the name of Jesus every knee shall bow and every tongue confess that He is Lord (Philippians 2:10).

Many believers all over the world are witnessing miracles when they call upon the name of Jesus in their moments of desperation. Untold lives have been transformed by the power in the name of Jesus. He is the same yesterday, today, and forever (Hebrews 13:8). Tell us who else died on the cross that we might live (1 Thessalonians 5:10)? And is there another who can claim the title Alpha and Omega, the Beginning and the End, the First and the Last (Revelation 22:13)? We say "Creator," and He knows we are talking about Him (John 1:1; Genesis 1:1).

When we say Counselor, Mighty God, or Prince of Peace, He is aware of whom we speak (Isaiah 9:6). Any time we cry Saviour and Lord in adoration He knows that we are worshipping Him (Romans 10:9). He is the only name under heaven whereby man can be saved (Acts 4:12). He is the way, the truth, and the life (John 14:6). He is the only King of Kings and Lord of Lords (Revelation 19:16). He is Jesus, the Resurrection and the Life (John 11:25). We worship you Jesus!

Where would I be without the Lord?

It's only fitting that I take this time to thank the Lord for everything that He has done in my life, in spite of me. I thank You Father for showing me grace and forgiveness instead of punishment and eternal banishment from your presence. Lord, thank you for a love that worked through the blood of Jesus to transform my life from a mess into a testimony of "How great thou art."

Yes, Lord my soul sings out loud this morning because like the psalmist in Psalm 3:4, "I cried unto the Lord with my voice, and he heard me out of his holy hill. Selah." Now, my prayer O God is that others like me would hear your voice and not harden their hearts but would call upon you in their distress. Your word says in John 6:37 that You will not reject anyone who comes to You; and Romans 10:13 states that whosoever calls on the name of the Lord shall be saved.

Friend, family, whosoever, if you do not know the Lord and are tired of a lifestyle without the direction of the Holy Spirit, turn to Jesus today (read Romans 10:9–13). He will, by His Spirit change your course and lead you into the path of grace—peace with God.

The reason for our hope

"But sanctify (honor) the Lord God in your hearts: and be ready always to give an answer to every man that asketh you a reason of the hope that is in you with meekness and fear" (1 Peter 3:15).

Do you know the reason for the hope that is in you—the reason why God chose you, saved you, delivered you, and gave you a "New name written down in glory?" Being cognizant of the fact that we were lost and Jesus found us, were blind but now we are able to see (spiritually), should give us hope for the future. The songwriter said "My hope is built on nothing less than Jesus blood and righteousness… On Christ the solid rock I stand, all other ground is sinking sand…" Child of God, on that sweet refrain, we follow that we are able to withstand, absorb like a top-class suspension system, whatever the world dishes out to us without fear or concern. Why? Because we are standing on a firm foundation, and nothing can harm us. The word of God states "the eyes of the Lord are over the righteous, and his ears are open unto their prayers" (1 Peter 3:12). Thus, we have an explanation for anyone who would like to know why we remain calm when those around us are hyperventilating. That is the reason why we bless them who curse us and pray for them who despitefully use us. Yes, man and woman of God, we should be ready to give a reason for our hope.

Where does the need for God fit into our "Hierarchy of Needs"?

"As the deer pants for streams of water, so I long for you, O God" (Psalm 42:1, NLT).

From conception to the grave, humans have needs; and depending on whom one talks to, one will discover that some needs are more important or prioritized at a higher level than others. According to Maslow's Hierarchy of Needs, at the lowest level of the hierarchy, we have the need for food, water, clothing, shelter, sex, and so forth—the very basic (physiological) needs. At the second level, we have "safety needs" which include the need for "security, employment, health and welfare, family, moralityand so forth." Third up the pyramid, we have the "belongingness and love needs—work groups, family, and so on."

Fourth up the hierarchy, we have "esteem needs" which include "self-esteem, achievement, mastery, independence, status, and dominance." And at the top of the hierarchy are the "self-actualization needs—realizing personal potential, self-fulfillment, seeking personal growth, and peak experiences." Maslow postulates that we all strive to satisfy the basic needs first.

But the question is where does the need for God fit into our "hierarchy of needs?" Can we honestly say that God is our first priority; recognized and sought after as our source for spiritual power and survival? Acts 17:28 (NLT) declares, "For in him we live and move and exist" which means that our need for the Spirit of God surpasses all other needs—without Him we are hopeless and powerless. The Psalmist in our text compares his need for the replenishing and resurrecting power of God with a deer panting after water.

According to the author of the article "Hunting Water Sources for Whitetail Deer," "Deer like all living things require water in order to survive. In the winter the deer requires about 1 1/2 quarts for every 100 pounds of body weight per day. In the warmer months they require about twice that much water." The deer needs plenty of water to survive; likewise we need the Spirit of God to survive. Jesus cried out in John 7:37–38 "If any man thirst let him come unto me, and drink. He that believeth on me, as the scripture hath said, out of his belly shall flow rivers of living water." We need Holy Ghost power.

Child of God, satisfy, if you will, the needs theorized by Maslow in his hierarchy, and there still remains a need that only water from the well of the Spirit of God can satisfy. Jesus spoke to the Samaritan woman about the need for this water in John 4:13–14, "Everyone who drinks of this water will be thirsty again, but those who drink of the water that I will give them will never be thirsty. The water that I will give will become in them a spring of water gushing up to eternal life." Friend, where does the need for God fit into our "hierarchy of needs?"

True worshippers

But the hour is coming, and now is, when the true worshipers will worship the Father in spirit and truth; for the Father is seeking such to worship Him. God *is* Spirit, and those who worship Him must worship in spirit and truth" (John 4:23–24).

Man was created in the image of God to worship Him (Genesis 1). Since the fall of Adam (Genesis 3), man has been searching for a replacement to fill the spiritual emptiness left in his heart. Like the Samaritan woman (the woman at the well), some of us have sought fulfillment in sexual gratification, not realizing that our seemingly unquenchable thirst can only be satiated by reconnecting to the source of our spiritual life—the living water springing up into everlasting life (John 4:7–14). Others have sought completeness in the worship of the idols of fame, fortune, jobs, professions, and even church attendance and meaningless work toward salvation.

Jesus is saying that true worship can only be attained when we have been brought back into a right relationship with the Father and have received power to become sons and daughters of God (John 1:12–13). True worshippers are those who have been reconciled with God through Christ Jesus, the source of grace and truth (2 Corinthians 5:17–21; John 1:17). God is looking for true worshippers today; folks who desire to walk in freedom, reflecting the glorious image of their Father (2 Corinthians 3:18).

Child of God, outward show alone is not enough. The word of God says that man looks at the outward appearance but God sees the heart (1 Samuel 16:7). The Lord knows those who are His; 2 Timothy 2:19 puts it "Nevertheless the foundation of God standeth sure, having this seal, The Lord knoweth them that are his. And, Let every one that nameth the name of Christ depart from iniquity."

True worshippers are not perfect people but are committed to become mature in the things of God (Matthew 5:48). True worshippers, according to Psalm 15:2 are "those who lead blameless lives and do what is right, speaking the truth from sincere hearts." True worshippers worship God "in spirit and truth."

The world needs our salt today

"You are the salt of the earth. But what good is salt if it has lost its flavor? Can you make it useful again? It will be thrown out and trampled underfoot as worthless" (Matthew 5:13, NLT).

Have you ever thought about the reason or reasons Jesus compared the influence of Christians in society to that of salt in the earth? Well, according to the Salt Institute, salt has over 14,000 uses due to its chemical and physical properties. Salt is important to life on earth. To underscore its importance, suffice it to say that wars have been fought over access to salt.

Worldwide, approximately forty percent of salt is used to make chlorine and soda ash, "the foundation of inorganic chemistry." Salt provides the nutritional base in foods given to livestock and poultry. In addition, most of us are familiar with the daily uses for salt in our homes. We use salt to cure meats and fish and to give a distinct flavor to our food in cooking. People tend to squirm and become depressed when told by a physician to lower or terminate their salt intake. Frankly, some foods have no flavor without salt. Can you imagine life without salt? Or worse, being provided salt that has no flavor?

Salt that has lost its flavor, for all practical purposes is useless. Jesus is saying in Matthew 5:13 that Christians should be the change agents in society. We've been imbued with Holy Ghost power and therefore, possess the cure for the world's ills. We have the life-saving nutrients for a dying world—the solution to the world's problems. We have Jesus, the "Balm of Gilead," the One who said "I have come that they might have life and that they might have it more abundantly" (John 10:10).

Yes, child of God, we are the salt of the earth; but if we are to remain useful and effective we must stay connected to our source (John 15:4). We must study the word of God, pray without ceasing, and be led by the Holy Spirit (2 Timothy 2:15; 1 Thessalonians 5:17; Romans 8:14). We ought to be prepared and ready to lead others to Christ; heal the sick and bring deliverance to those who are in bondage (Mark 16:15–18). But if we have lost our flavor it means that we have become weak, impotent believers and consequently, of no value in the earth. Friends, the world needs salt; let's stay strong in the Lord.

Who do you present to the world?

John 1:36 " .... Behold the Lamb of God!"

How do you react when mistreated by your friend, boss, spouse or harassed by the driver in the other car on the road way? Have you ever given someone a piece of your mind or a good pummeling and perhaps were justified in doing so under the world's standards but felt remorseful afterwards? That's because we know instinctively that our lives should reflect a certain Christ-likeness commensurate with our profession of faith.

It's very easy to buckle under the pressures of life and behave in ways that cloud our witness for Christ. But as children of the Most High God, we have been endowed with the responsibility of shining the light of truth into men's lives. We are the beneficiaries of grace and truth with a commission to present Jesus Christ, the Lamb of God to the entire world. Who do you present to the world? Will they be able to "behold the Lamb of God" in your life today?

Can you see Him in the storm?

It's difficult sometimes to recognize Jesus in the middle of your raging storm and tempest. But He is saying the same thing to you today as He said to His frightened disciples on the wind tossed waves, on their way to the other side: "Be of good cheer; it is I, be not afraid" (Matthew 14:27). Child of God, Jesus will never leave us alone in any situation. Don't allow the chaos around you to cloud your vision of our Deliverer's presence. Look with the eyes of faith. Can you see Him in the storm?

I don't have to see to believe

"...for we walk by faith, not by sight" (2 Corinthians 5:7).

It's easy to believe when you have seen or are able to see, but it takes faith to believe when you have not seen or are unable to see. Stepping out into unknown, uncharted territory based on a word from God demands faith. Abraham made the "Hall of Faith" for doing that very thing (Hebrews 11). Believing that your present circumstance will change in your favor while dark clouds blur your vision takes faith. Joseph spent fourteen years contemplating his fate after dreams of elevation and success before he was summoned to the palace (Genesis 37, 39, 40, 41).

It takes faith to spend years interceding for a lost loved one, maybe a prodigal child, when the odds against his or her return seems less in your favor as each day goes by. Noah preached 120 years to his lost generation while building the ark, based on a word from God—even though he had no idea what the word rain meant. Habakkuk 2:4 says that "The just shall live by faith" which means that our life of righteousness in Christ is a walk guided by the authority of God's word. Jesus said in John 20:29, "Blessed are those who believe without seeing me." My friend, I don't know about you but I don't have to see to believe.

If we lose our life, we save it—one of the paradoxes of faith in Christ

In Luke 9:24 Jesus said, "For whoever will save his life shall lose it: but whoever will lose his life for my sake, the same shall save it."

The paradox here is that if we truly want to live the abundant life in Christ, we must give up our lives, our own will for God's "will" to "be done on earth as it is in heaven" (Matthew 6:10). Our pride and selfish ambitions must give way to the leading of the Spirit of God. When we have made the decision to accept Jesus as savior and Lord of our lives, we have, in essence given control over to His Lordship and have become His workmanship (Ephesians 2:10).

We are no longer captains of our own souls, now our "anchor holds and grips the solid Rock"—Jesus. The Apostle Paul puts it this way in Colossians 3:3 (NLT), "For you died to this life, and your real life is hidden with Christ in God." We use to sing an old hymn that says in part "Where He leads me I will follow; I'll go with Him all the way." We may not know ahead of time where our faith in Christ will take us but we can be sure of one thing and that is, our willingness to lose our lives paves the way for eternal security in Him.

This new life, contrary to a popular teaching, may not always bring material wealth and comfort here on earth, as a matter of fact, we may face trouble, conflict, turmoil; and sail through many storms and tempests. But the word of God states in Hebrews 13:5, "*Let your* conduct *be* without covetousness; *be* content with such things as you have. For He Himself has said, "I will never leave you nor forsake you." Child of God, this Christian walk is all about dying to self, for each one of us must lose our life if we are to save it (idea taken from Answer.com).

"But as for me and my house"

Joshua 24:15 "And if it seem evil unto you to serve the Lord, choose you this day whom ye will serve; whether the gods which your fathers served that were on the other side of the flood, or the gods of the Amorites, in whose land ye dwell: but as for me and my house, we will serve the Lord."

We are living in an age where biblical truths are systematically being attacked by an anti-God element in our society bent on dismissing all absolutes. Their objective is to shroud any distinctions between good and evil, right and wrong with spurious arguments (Isaiah 5:20). Behaviors that were once universally condemned because they were considered deviant and unnatural are not only socially acceptable today but have been catapulted into the same legal status as civil rights. Cultural diversity advocates while seeking to coerce and cajole everyone into buying into certain lifestyle choices, no matter how repulsive to a majority of Bible-believing citizens, have been successful in painting anyone who dissents or disagrees with their agenda as intolerant (see Jude 1:7; John 3:19–21).

How times have changed! Men and women of God dare not preach against certain sins or moral decadence for fear of attracting the wrath of a very powerful, wealthy, and influential minority lobby (see 2 Timothy 3:1–17). Where do we go from here? Who do we obey, God or man? Are the true followers of Christ, the remnant ready to be thrown once more into the fiery furnaces of the prevailing culture or prepared to become food for lions in the dens of iniquity and abomination? See Matthew 24:9.

The proverbial line has been drawn in the sand; one may either put on the whole armor of God, take a stand (in love), or bow under the pressure and receive the mark of the beast (Revelation 13:16–18). But the time has come for all those who are called by the name of the Lord to choose this day who they will serve. Like Joshua, let our response be: "As for me and my house, we will serve the Lord."

Time to move over to Faith-ville

"What is faith? It is the confident assurance that what we hope for is going to happen. It is the evidence of things we cannot yet see" (Hebrews 11:1, NLT).

Webster's College Dictionary defines faith as "belief that is not based on proof." In other words, if one is from the "show me" state of mind or the "believe it when I see it" doubting community, one will be very uncomfortable in Faith-ville.

In Faith-ville, we believe that everything is possible with God (Matthew 19:26). In our neighborhood, people seek after God and meditate on His word day and night (Psalm 1). Residents of our town place complete confidence (trust) in the God of Abraham, Isaac, and Jacob, believing that we are justified by faith in Jesus Christ (Romans 5:1). Further, we know, unlike the people of "show me" and "believe it when I see it," without faith it is impossible to please God (Hebrews 11:6).

We the believers from Faith-ville, have awakened today with renewed vigor and hope, knowing that mercies are new and God's compassion will not fail us (Lamentations 3:22–23). We know that, in spite of the negative reports or prognoses, financial obstacles, wayward husbands or wives, intransigent children, or difficulty in the professional arena, God will work it out for our good (Romans 8:28). The people of Faith-ville do not have to see the proof to believe God and obey Him.

Finally, we invite all doubters to come over to Faith-ville, where we recognize that the battle is the Lord's and that if we just stand still, we shall see the salvation of the Lord (2 Chronicles 20:17). Take a leap of faith and experience what it is like to be sons and daughters of God, being led by the Spirit of God (Romans 8:14). Friend, if you are tired of life in "show me" and "believe it when I see it" move over to Faith-ville.

Following Christ

Matthew 4:20, "And they straightway left their nets, and followed him." My friends, I would like you to think on the following questions: (1) who are you following? (2) Why are you following? (3) Have you counted the cost?

If the answer to question number one is any person other than Jesus Christ, you may want to revisit the Gospels (Matthew, Mark, Luke, and John). Assuming that you are following Jesus, the reason for following (question #2) should be, to become disciples of Christ and ultimately, "fishers of men" (Matthew 4:19). Many are following for titles and positions, for wealth and status, for reasons that according to the word, could lead to these words from Christ, "depart from me workers of iniquity, I never knew you."

Finally, what will it cost to follow or serve the Lord? It will cost us everything. Following Jesus Christ means self-sacrifice. It means being led by the Spirit of God, mortifying the deeds of the flesh, and giving up our selfish rights for the cause of Christ. It means being attacked and abused at times for our faith.

Following Christ for the right reasons will cost us something, saints. But the good news is that although we are paying a high cost to follow Christ, the rewards of this kingdom life are immeasurable. We get to spread the gospel and witness sinners being saved by God's grace. We have his divine protection. The Lord supplies all our needs according to His riches in glory. We have an expected end—we shall see the King in all His glory.

Let's become the unified Body of Christ

> For as we have many members in one body and all members have not the same office: so we, being many, are one body in Christ, and every one members one of another. Having then gifts differing according to the grace that is given to us, whether prophecy, let us prophesy according to the proportion of faith; Or ministry, let us wait on our ministering: or he that

teacheth, on teaching; Or he that exhorteth, on exhortation: he that giveth, let him do it with simplicity; he that ruleth, with diligence; he that sheweth mercy, with cheerfulness. Let love be without dissimulation. Abhor that which is evil; cleave to that which is good (Romans 12:4–9).

As we mature in the things of the Lord, it should have become quite evident that each one of us has been blessed with certain gifts and talents that are unique to us. Here we are in the Body of Christ, many members from different backgrounds, with a kaleidoscope of talents and gifts trying to carve out our own niche. The question is how do we stay unified, each member understanding that in order for the body to function as a well-conducted orchestra, everyone has to play his or her part with focus and dedication?

The soloist must be of the understanding that the conductor is in charge and that each part, whether blended into the sound or allowed momentarily to shine above the rest, should remain devoted to the conductor's vision and the proper interpretation of the music. The piano has its part to play and so does the violin; both are equally important. Whenever we get to the point in the concert where the instruments start competing with each other or refusing to play at all, then we will have become dysfunctional.

Child of God, we ought to be working together in love, as one body of Christ. Our conductor is the Holy Spirit, and He leads us according to the word of God. If there is confusion, folks, we know the Lord is not involved because He is not a God of confusion (1 Corinthians 14:33). There is one Lord, one faith and one baptism (Ephesians 4:5). Let's play our part well but with the knowledge that we are His instruments here on earth, adopted into the household of Christ to play the same tune: to preach the gospel of Jesus Christ to the world.

God wrote the score, and we all must play as one unit. The following scriptures are provided for further reference:

1 Corinthians 12:12, "Just as a body, though one, has many parts, but all its many parts form one body, so it is with Christ."

Ephesians 4:4, There is one body and one Spirit, just as you were called to one hope when you were called; "

Ephesians 4:16, "From him the whole body, joined and held together by every supporting ligament, grows and builds itself up in love, as each part does its work."

Are you equipped to respond appropriately?

"Everyone enjoys a fitting reply; it is wonderful to say the right thing at the right time" (Proverbs 15:23, NLT),

Many people are searching for answers to some of life's perplexing questions, most of which only the Spirit of God through his infinite wisdom can provide. The anti-God sentiment being fueled by a small minority notwithstanding, most folks are looking to the church and believers, Christ's ambassadors, for help. To be of any meaningful assistance, every child of God ought to appreciate this great responsibility; begin to study the scriptures, pray continuously, and earnestly seek the Lord. Then, and only then, will we be able to speak truthfully into the lives of those who are desperate for a word from the Lord. Are you equipped to respond appropriately?

My God is real

Psalm 53:1 "The fool hath said in his heart, there is no God. Corrupt are they, and have done abominable iniquity: there is none that doeth good."

There should be no doubt in anyone's mind, as to the existence of a God who created everything, formed man and breathed life into him. The word of God is saying that only a fool says that there is no God because creation itself attests to the existence of a wise, proactive, and loving God. The Psalmist wrote in Psalm 19:1, "The heavens declare the glory of God; and the firmament sheweth his handiwork."

Today, please take a moment to pause with me and give reverence to our great and mighty God, who is our Creator and awesome Ruler. He kept us through the night; woke us up this morning; and clothed us in our right minds. Let's glorify our God who gives grace to the humble but resists the proud (James 4:6). Child of God now is a good time to sing with conviction, the old hymn written by Kenneth Morris, "My God is real":

Verse 1:
There are some things I may not know,
there are some places I cannot go;
but I am sure of this one thing,
that God is real for I can feel Him deep within.

Chorus:
Yes, God is real,
real in my soul.
Yes, God is real
for He has washed and made me whole.
His love for me is like pure gold,
yes, God is real
for I can feel Him in my soul.

Lord, send laborers

And Jesus went about all the cities and villages, teaching in their synagogues, and preaching the gospel of the kingdom, and healing every sickness and every disease among the people. But when he saw the multitudes, he was moved with compassion on them, because they fainted, and were scattered abroad, as sheep having no shepherd. Then saith he unto his disciples, "The harvest truly is plenteous, but the labourers are few; Pray ye therefore the Lord of the harvest, that he will send forth labourers into his harvest. (Matthew 9:35–38)

If you are as concerned today, as Jesus was and still is, please pray with me.

Father God, you are holy, righteous and worthy of all praise. We honor and glorify your name today. We ask that you send us laborers who are willing to go into every nation, city, village, and hamlet to reap this mighty harvest of souls for your kingdom. It is evident that the people are still faint and scattered abroad, as sheep without a shepherd; and sickness and diseases have reached epidemic proportions. We need laborers, anointed with Holy Ghost power to teach in our churches, preach the gospel of the kingdom, and heal the people of their maladies. We thank you for the few who have been toiling in their various capacities to fulfill the great commission, but we need more Christians who will answer the call and say "Here I am Lord, send me!" Open the eyes of your people to the needs and desperation of their neighbors next door and inspire a great movement of believers who will labor for the cause of Christ. Lord, send laborers, in the name of Jesus. We thank you, Lord. Amen!

We are very special to Him

If you woke up this morning feeling like you can't measure up to other people's expectations of you, that you are not good enough, snap out of it. The devil is a liar. What does God say about you? Psalm 139:14 states "I will praise thee; for I am fearfully and wonderfully made: marvelous are thy works; and that my soul knoweth right well." Yes, friend, we are God's marvelous work. Remember the Oscar-nominated movie, *The Help*? The main character, Aibileen reminded the child of an abusive employer on a daily basis that: "You are smart; you are beautiful; and you are important." Child of God, tell your soul that you are the apple of God's eye and that God loved you enough to send Jesus to die for you. Hallelujah! We are very special to the Lord.

Praise the Lord, family and friends! The grave could not hold our Lord and Savior; Jesus is risen indeed!

1 Corinthians 15:55, "O death, where is your sting? O grave, where is your victory?"

Romans 4:25, "He was delivered over to death for our sins and was raised to life for our justification."

1 Corinthians 15:17, 20–22, "And if Christ has not been raised, then your faith is useless and you are still guilty of your sins. But now is Christ risen from the dead, and become the first fruits of them that slept. For since by man came death, by man came also the resurrection of the dead. For as in Adam all die, even so in Christ shall all be made alive."

Hallelujah! We serve a living Savior: He is King of Kings and Lord of Lords, Conquering Lion of the tribe of Judah—Jesus the Christ.

Call upon Jesus today

"For whosoever shall call upon the name of the Lord shall be saved" (Romans 10:13).

I'm so thankful that God's grace is available to "whosoever" and that all we have to do is call upon Jesus to access the gift of salvation. Friend, it does not matter who we are or what we have done; the Lord will not turn a deaf ear to anyone who calls upon him with a broken and a contrite heart (Psalm 51:17). The name of Jesus is powerful and mighty enough to save us from our wretchedness. Call upon Jesus today!

Chapter Five

MORE WISDOM NUGGETS

To live for Jesus Christ is to live by faith

"What is faith? It is the confident assurance that what we hope for is going to happen. It is the evidence of things we cannot yet see" (Hebrews 11:1 NLT). It takes faith to believe that God spoke the universe into existence (verse 2). It is by faith that we accept the free gift of salvation provided by Christ's shed blood on Calvary's cross. We need faith to live a victorious life, to enjoy the promises of God, as the seed of Abraham. The question then is how do we acquire faith? Romans 10:17 (NLT) tells us that "Faith comes from listening to this message of good news, the Good News about Christ."

Friend, if we are not living by faith, we are in rebellion against God. Hebrews 11:6 (NLT) declares "…it is impossible to please God without faith. Anyone who wants to come to him must believe that there is a God and that he rewards those who sincerely seek him." Romans 1:17 tells us that "the just shall live by faith." Child of God, you may not know where the next meal is coming from, but by faith you and yours will be fed. The school fees may be due and the bank account empty, but God will provide. You may not have all the qualifications for that high-paying job, but God said it's yours. Whose report are you going to believe? Faith in God leads us to believe what the word says about us and causes us to look in anticipation for our miracle.

Faith says "There is nothing too hard for God" (Jeremiah 32:17). Faith says that "He is the same yesterday, today and forever" (Hebrews 13:8). Faith says that God honors His word above his name therefore; if He said it we will believe it. Faith says the righteous will not be forsaken neither will his seed beg bread (Psalm 37:25). Faith says "No weapon formed against us shall prosper, and every tongue that shall rise against us in judgment we shall condemn" (Isaiah 54:17). Faith says we don't have to see it to believe it because "we walk by faith and not by sight" (2 Corinthians 5:7). To live for Jesus is to live by faith. Have faith in God and prosper.

Let's be productive, fruitful believers

According to the Apostle Peter, "By his divine power, God has given us everything we need for living a godly life. We have received all of this by coming to know him, the one who called us to himself by means of his marvelous glory and excellence. And because of his glory and excellence, he has given us great and precious promises. These are the promises that enable you to share his divine nature and escape the world's corruption caused by human desires. In view of all this, make every effort to respond to God's promises. Supplement your faith with a generous provision of moral excellence, and moral excellence with knowledge, and knowledge with self-control, and self-control with patient endurance, and patient endurance with godliness, and godliness with brotherly affection, and brotherly affection with love for everyone. The more you grow like this, the more productive and useful you will be in your knowledge of our Lord Jesus Christ. But those who fail to develop in this way are shortsighted or blind, forgetting that they have been cleansed from their old sins. So, dear brothers and sisters, work hard to prove that you really are among those God has called and chosen. Do these things and you will never fall away. Then God will give you a grand entrance into the eternal Kingdom of our Lord and Savior Jesus Christ." (2 Peter 1:3–11, NLT).

What kind of children are we raising?

"Train up a child in the way he should go: and when he is old, he will not depart from it" (Proverbs 22:6).

Many parents from my generation have watched with dismay, as a new breed of children surfaced with a new attitude of defiance and rebelliousness. Mostly, these are the children who have literally raised themselves (latch-key kids), have spent countless hours watching television programs not suited for adults; playing video games that would scare most folks over thirty; and who lack basic social skills. Some have everything given to them, while others are less fortunate. Their mothers and fathers have either divorced or were never married, and nine times out of ten, the children were raised by a working single parent.

The foundation of the family structure has been broken down, and in the absence of parental, godly guidance, the children of this generation seem lost, cold, and in some cases, very callous. The Bible warns that we should train up a child in the right way if we desire to have a sober adult. Training implies guidance and a routine to achieve a specified outcome; which means that parents have been given the arduous task of molding and shaping their children to be wise and productive social beings. There is no doubt that the children of today are unbelievably technologically savvy but most lack the fundamentals of love, compassion, and respect for adults and authority.

The question then is what kind of children are we raising? Are they the young men of inner city Chicago and Philadelphia, blowing each other's brains all over the pavements of their concrete jungles or the rude boys from the inner city streets of lush Caribbean islands? Maybe they are the mass murderers that have been plaguing the lush green gentrified suburbs of middle – and upper middle-class America, such as Newtown, Connecticut.

What kind of children are we raising? While not all of these children have resorted to violence and murder, the point is that far too many young people have become the products of an uncaring, me-centered, morally bankrupt, empty culture. In this modern, Hollywood-directed culture, many parents have abdicated their responsibilities and have allowed the god of this world to usurp the scriptural, God-centered teachings of right and wrong. Should we be surprised that some children, who have been raised in this way, are inoculated against sensitivity and love and are now Zombies of evil, to be feared by even the parents themselves?

The Apostle Paul lamented the condition of the society of his day, when he stated in Romans 1:28-32:

> And even as they did not like to retain God in their knowledge, God gave them over to a reprobate mind, to do those things which are not convenient; being filled with all unrighteousness, fornication, wickedness, covetousness, maliciousness; full of envy, murder, strife, deceit, malignity; whisperers, backbiters, haters of God, despiteful, proud, boasters, inventors of evil things, disobedient to parents, without understanding, covenant-breakers, without natural affection, implacable, unmerciful: who knowing the judgment of God, that they which commit such things are worthy of death, not only do the same, but have pleasure in them that do them.

Parents, our children are our responsibility, and the Lord will hold us responsible for the way in which we have raised them. We cannot afford to give up parental control to Hollywood, television, video games and technology, and the prevailing culture and absolve ourselves of our responsibility to train them up in the way of the word of God. Unless we are willing to watch as their lives play out like a scene from a horror movie. Friend, what kind of children are we raising? Joshua 24:15 says "As for me and my house, we will serve the Lord."

Whose report do you believe?

"Who has believed our message? To whom has the LORD revealed his powerful arm?" (Isaiah 53:1, NLT) Note the KJV, "Who hath believed our report? And to whom is the arm of the LORD revealed?"

I don't care how many prognosticators have told you that your situation is hopeless; the word of God says that there is nothing too hard for God (Jeremiah 32:17). The plan of the adversary is to misdirect your focus from God to your problem. His calculated attacks are designed to steal, kill, and destroy—your health, safety and overall prosperity, especially financially.

The medical report may have left you embracing a future of pain and suffering, but I've come to let you know that "He was wounded for our transgressions, he was bruised for our iniquities: the chastisement of our peace was upon him; and with his stripes we were healed" (Isaiah 53:5). Choose to believe the Lord, and He will heal your body like He has done for countless others. Reach out and touch the hem of His garment right now by faith, and He will do for you what he did for the woman with the issue of blood (Luke 8:43).

Your enemy may have been causing you anxiety and sleepless nights however, I decree and declare: "Let God arise, let his enemies be scattered," in Jesus name (Psalm 68:1). Child of God, "No weapon formed against thee shall prosper; and every tongue that shall rise against thee in judgment thou shall condemn." The Bible says in Deuteronomy 28:7: "The Lord shall cause your enemies who rise up against you to be defeated before your face; they shall come out against you one way and flee before you seven ways."

When the financial report indicates doom and gloom, comfort yourself by telling your circumstance "The Lord is my shepherd; I shall not want. He maketh me to lie down in green pastures: he leadeth me beside the still waters." Philippians 4:19 states "But my God shall supply all your need according to His riches in glory by Christ Jesus." Remember, God promises wealth and riches to the household of the generation of the righteous (Psalm 112:3).

My friend, whose report do you believe? I don't know about you but as for me and God's people, we choose to believe the report of the Lord. I pray that the Lord will bless you, from the crown of your head to the soles of your feet in Jesus' mighty name.

Have a thankful day

Today, I don't know about you but all I want to do is thank my Lord for His goodness and love toward me. Psalm 107:1 (NLT) declares "Give thanks to the LORD, for he is good! His faithful love endures forever." Hallelujah! Sometimes we ought to forget about our wants and desires and just thank our God and King. If one looks over one's life with a grateful heart, it ought to be quite easy to say "Thank you Lord."

Church, do you want the glory of God to come down in a real way? Let's begin to dedicate whole services to do nothing but thank, praise and adore the God of our salvation like the people did in 2 Chronicles 5:13 "The trumpeters and musicians joined in unison to give praise and thanks to the LORD. Accompanied by trumpets, cymbals and other instruments, the singers raised their voices in praise to the LORD and sang: "He is good; his love endures forever." Then the temple of the LORD was filled with the cloud."

Thank you, Lord

"O give thanks unto the Lord; for he is good; for his mercy endureth for ever" (1 Chronicles 16:34).

Father God, with grateful hearts we thank you for being God: for being good and merciful all the time. Thank you for salvation, paid for by the shed blood of Jesus Christ and allocated to us by grace through faith. For your love toward us, thank you, Lord.

Abba, for the air we breathe, thank you; for the food we eat, thank you; for clothing, shelter, and security, thank you, Lord. For family, friends and the people you have placed strategically in our lives to help us along the way, thank you. For wisdom and understanding, thank you, Lord. For your peace and a mind to serve you, thank you, Lord. Lord, in everything we give you thanks; in the precious name of Jesus (Jeshu'a).

Are you stressed out trying to be righteous?

That we are incapable of appeasing God with our good works is a foregone conclusion, according to the word of God. Therefore, understanding that we are the righteousness of God through the finished work of Jesus Christ on the cross, will deliver us from the anxieties associated with our efforts to be righteous. There are a number of scripture references indicating that our righteousness falls under the purview of God via our Lord and Savior Jesus Christ.

Romans 3:22, states, "We are made right with God by placing our faith in Jesus Christ. And this is true for everyone who believes, no matter who we are." And 2 Corinthians 5:21

affirms "God made him who had no sin to be sin for us, so that in him we might become the righteousness of God." In addition, Isaiah 64:6 says in part, "We are all as an unclean thing, and all our righteousnesses are as filthy rags."In other words, any attempt by sinful man to be righteous before God will prove futile.

Friends, we are safe and secure in the love of God, covered under the blood of the Lamb. Rest in God's grace and walk in the liberty bequeath to us at Calvary.

Are your dreams big enough to attract dream-killers?

"And they said one to another, Behold, this dreamer cometh" (Genesis 37:19). Friend, when God has placed big dreams in your heart, you'd better be prepared for a fight. Only big dreams attract jealousy and envy. Big dreams alert those around you that you are about to reach heights far beyond their imaginations and that your God is positioning you for a major blessing. Dream killers, whether you know it or not, are aware of your potential greatness by the size of your dreams. So, their main goal is to stop you from dreaming thereby preventing your predominance. Are your dreams big enough to attract dream-killers? Maybe it's time to ask the Lord to give you bigger dreams.

Be cautious

These six things doth the Lord hate: yea, seven are an abomination unto him: 17) A proud look, a lying tongue, and hands that shed innocent blood, 18) An heart that deviseth wicked imaginations, feet that be swift in running to mischief, 19) A false witness that speaketh lies, and he that soweth discord among brethren (Proverbs 6:16–19).

Be encouraged; there will be a time of joy and gladness

"Those who have been ransomed by the LORD will return. They will enter Jerusalem singing, crowned with everlasting joy. Sorrow and mourning will disappear, and they will be filled with joy and gladness" (Isaiah 35:10).

Revelation 7:17 says "For the Lamb at the center of the throne will be their shepherd; 'he will lead them to springs of living water.' 'And God will wipe away every tear from their eyes."

Revelation 21:4 also says "He will wipe every tear from their eyes. There will be no more death' or mourning or crying or pain, for the old order of things has passed away."

Let's be cheerful givers

"Don't give reluctantly or in response to pressure, for God loves the person who gives cheerfully. And God will generously provide all you need. Then you will always have everything you need and plenty left over to share with others" (2 Corinthians 9:7–8).

The word of God is admonishing us to develop an attitude of gratitude toward God by giving willingly to His work. Then we will experience His abundance to the degree that we will be able to bless others. Let's change our lives for the better by becoming cheerful givers.

God's word is enough to make us wise

Paul's letter to the Colossians states in 3:16 "Let the words of Christ, in all their riches, live in your hearts and make you wise. Use his words to teach and counsel each other."

There is a common thread running through the teachings of most cults that had their genesis in Christianity, that is, on their reliance on fanciful revelations independent of or in addition to the Bible. Most often, founders of these groups relied heavily on dreams and or visions that provided them with "wisdom" other than what one would normally derive from the inspired word of God. But the Apostle Paul is reminding us via his directive to the Colossian church that the words of Christ have all the wisdom we need "to teach and counsel each other." Friend, we don't need any more strange philosophies or spurious dreams and visions that scripture is unable to support; God's word is enough to make us wise.

Do not fall for their tricks

"Be sober, be vigilant; because your adversary the devil, as a roaring lion, walking about, seeking whom he may devour" (1 Peter 5:8).

Be especially careful of wolves in sheep's clothing pretending to be Christians. Satan, disguised as a friend will try to mislead and entrap the unsuspecting child of God. Some people are envious of the fact that God is using you in an uncommon way and will go to extremes in their scheme to derail and thereby disqualify you. But note: "Behold, the eye of the Lord is upon them that fear him, upon them that hope in his mercy" (Psalm 33:18).

How much do you need God?

"But as for me, it is good to be near God. I have made the Sovereign Lord my refuge; I will tell of all your deeds" (Psalm 73:28).

With each new day we should become more aware of our need for God and, like the Psalmist, stay near Him. Unlike the relationship with our natural parents where at a certain point in time we are expected to grow up and lose our childlike dependence, our attachment to our heavenly Father is expected to gain strength over time. We are never weaned from our Creator, and if we ever get to that place where we think cutting the spiritual umbilical cord proves our maturity, it may be time for another lesson in humility.

James 4:8 tells that we should draw near to God and He will draw near to us. Note that our Lord and Savior Jesus, the Christ kept a very close bond with God the Father, as evidenced by his constant prayer life (Luke 5:16). Jesus stayed in perpetual communion with His source of strength and so should we (Luke 18:1). The song writer said "I need thee, O I need thee; every hour I need thee...." Do you still need God?

Don't lose sight of the vision (no pun intended)

And the Lord answered me, and said, Write the vision, and make it plain upon tablets, that he may run that readeth it. For the vision is yet for an appointed time, but at the end it shall speak, and not lie: though it tarry, wait for it; because it will surely come, it will not tarry" (Habakkuk 2:2–3).

Friend, when God has supernaturally imprinted in your spirit, a plan for the future, concerning you, your family, a people, a nation, or nations, mark your calendar, write it down, put it on YouTube. It's a done deal. Now, wait with expectancy because "The strength of Israel will not lie nor repent." (1 Samuel 15:29). If He said it, you can bet your life on that word; it will come to pass.

Those who are spiritual among us will understand when I say metaphorically; remain pregnant in the spirit until the birthing canal opens, at the "appointed time." Some of you have received a word from the Lord, for what may seem like an eternity ago but, as sure as night follows the day, the vision will become reality. Be not overcome with doubt and fatigue; rest on the infallible, life-sustaining word of God. There will be naysayers, scoffers, the blind, and the lost, whose job it is to highjack and abort the vision. But child of God, Habakkuk says "it will surely come." Don't lose sight of the vision.

Go forth and be strong in the Lord

"Finally my brethren, be strong in the Lord, and in the power of his might" (Ephesians 6:10).

I'm sure many of you have heard fellow Christians make the following request of others in the church at one time or another: "Brother/sister, please pray for my strength in the Lord." But the question is, can anyone be the benefactor of strength in the Lord by simply asking someone else to pray? Is it possible to receive strength to fight the good fight by osmosis—having it seep into our spirit without personal sacrifice? By sacrifice I mean studying the word of truth, praying, fasting, and putting on the whole armor of God (Ephesians 6:11–18).

While all things are possible with God, scripture is clear on how Christians ought to engage our spiritual adversary on a daily basis. Yes, God's grace is sufficient and His strength is made perfect in weakness (according to the Apostle Paul), but ignoring a fervent prayer life, living like the devil, and abusing our position as children of the Most High will only make us fodder for the enemy of our souls. We need to pray for each other and do what we can to assist the personal and spiritual growth of others. However, none of us is exempt from our personal responsibility to seek the Lord and clothe ourselves with the whole armor of God (Ephesians 6:11).

There are times when we need to stand with our own loins girt about with truth; our own breastplate of righteousness; our own feet shod with the preparation of the gospel of peace; our own shield of faith; our own helmet of salvation; our own sword of the spirit (i.e., knowing the word for oneself); and be able to pray and watch for ourselves (Ephesians 6:14–18).

Friend, there are certain things no one will be able to do for us, if we desire to be strong in the Lord. Now, put on your whole armor; go forth and be strong in the Lord today!

God has promised mercy

> For the Lord hath called thee as a woman forsaken and grieved in spirit, and a wife of youth, when thou wast refused, saith thy God. For a small moment have I forsaken thee, but with great mercies will I gather thee. In a little wrath I hid my face from thee for a moment, but with everlasting kindness will I have mercy on thee, saith the Lord thy redeemer (Isaiah 54:6–8).

This passage of scripture was especially pacifying to me many years ago when failure was a constant companion and life seemed hopeless. However, you can rest assured, child of God, that whatever state or condition you are in, God has promised you mercy and restoration. Suffice it to say that the Lord will turn your mourning, sadness, marginalization, and hopelessness into a time of rejoicing and dancing—a time of thanksgiving.

My travailing friend, it's not over yet. You are loved, and the grace and mercy of God will bring you deliverance. Hold on to the promises of the God of Isaiah, the God of our Lord and Savior Jesus Christ. Young person, you are not alone; you are on God's mind. Yes, it may seem dark and hopeless but the God of Israel will intervene on your behalf. Remember, "Weeping may endure for a night but joy comes in the morning" (Psalm 30:5). God has promised mercy.

God will teach us to profit when He leads

"Thus saith the Lord, thy Redeemer, the Holy One of Israel; I am the Lord thy God which teacheth thee to profit, which leadeth thee by the way that thou shouldest go" (Isaiah 48:17). The song writer said "Where He leads me I will follow. I'll go with Him all the way." Let's follow Jesus all the way and prosper.

Accept what Jesus did on the cross and become the righteousness of God

"For he had made him to be sin for us, who knew no sin; that we might be made the righteousness of God in him" (2 Corinthians 5:21). Friend, we can never work hard enough to become righteous. Only through the shed blood of Jesus can we claim to be God's righteousness. May grace and peace be multiplied to us!

The word of God is sweet

Psalm 119:103 "How sweet your words taste to me; they are sweeter than honey." I love the words of God because they guide and make me wiser than my enemies; they give me more insight than my teachers; living by them gives me greater wisdom than my elders; and they allow me to resist and keep from doing evil. The Spirit of God has taught me well and I will not turn away . Now you understand why God's words are sweeter than honey. (Read also, verses 98-102)

"Nothing can separate us from God's love."

Whatever you're faced with today be mindful of the fact that the Lord loves you beyond measure. Romans 8:38-39 states:

> And I am convinced that nothing can ever separate us from his love. Death can't, and life can't. The angels can't, and the demons can't. Our fears for today, our

worries about tomorrow, and even the powers of hell can't keep God's love away. Whether we are high above the sky or in the deepest ocean, nothing in all creation will ever be able to separate us from the love of God that is revealed in Christ Jesus our Lord.

Guided by truth

"When the Spirit of truth comes, he will guide you into all truth. He will not be presenting his own ideas; he will be telling you what he has heard. He will tell you about the future" (John 16:13).

Interestingly, at the end of all the Presidential Debates the fact checkers went into high gear, researching the veracity of the candidates' statements. Most reasonable people would agree that truth does matter, even in politics. An obscure Christian educator once admonished his students "Be transparent! Facades soon decay, exposing the truth anyway." Tell it now or be found out later—the truth will be revealed in time.

Friends, as children of the Most High God it is imperative that we walk in truth. We ought not to be misled by falsehoods and half-truths prevalent in today's culture. The Spirit of truth has given us a unique perspective and made us the prophetic voice of truth in our generation. We should be the "go to" folks in both public and private arenas because of our access to this vast reservoir of knowledge and truth coming from the Holy Spirit. Speak as the oracle of God, guided by truth. Be blessed!

We are shining lights

"Let your light so shine before men, that they may see your good works, and glorify your Father which is in heaven" (Matthew 5:16).

Let's resolve to be all that God wants us to be today; and shine brightly as men and women of God. Let's brighten someone's day with a smile so wide and joyful that the atmosphere becomes infected with happiness. Let our love for Jesus be so contagious that family, friends, coworkers, business partners, and everyone with whom we come in contact will see Christ in us the hope of glory. Let's be the good Samaritans of our communities and provide assistance to the least among us. Let's be the light in every dark nook and cranny of this earth today, so that others may come to know the Light of our salvation.

We are triumphant

"And having spoiled principalities and powers, he made a show of them openly, triumphing over them in it." (Colossians 2:15).

Child of God, the battle is already won. Jesus decimated the enemy therefore, greater is He that is in us than he that is in the world (1 John 4:4). Let's go forth today with confidence in the name above every other name (Philippians 2:9). Praise His Holy name—Jesus!

Overcomers

My son, forget not my law; but let thine heart keep my commandments: 2 For length of days, and long life, and peace, shall they add to thee. 3 Let not mercy and truth forsake thee: bind them about thy neck; write them upon the table of thine heart: 4 So shalt thou find favour and good understanding in the sight of God and man (Proverbs 3:1–4).

Having favor with God and man and enjoying a blameless reputation can be ours today. The only requirement is that we walk according to the God's directions, as laid out in His word. We can enjoy prosperous, full and peaceful lives with great reputations if we follow the leading of the Holy Spirit and allow truth and mercy to guide all our transactions, relationships, and ministries. Let's be overcomers, vessels of honor in the kingdom of God.

Have you ever overstayed your welcome in a certain season of your walk?

"To everything there is a season, and a time to every purpose under the heaven" (Ecclesiastes 3:1).

It's very easy to linger in a place, relationship, job, or anointing not knowing that the proverbial brook has dried up. That place where you saw progress and prosperity could very well become a place of frustration and even defeat if you do not understand that seasons change. The relationship which at first brought you joy and excitement could leave you tired and angry if you failed to heed the warning signs, clearly indicating the appropriate time to move on. Sometimes the job that brought you status and fulfillment will morph easily into a nightmare if you are unaware when the Lord has closed a particular door, in order to open a new one with bigger and better opportunities.

Finally, child of God, often times we become so rooted and grounded in an old anointing that we are rendered oblivious to the promptings of the Holy Spirit, telling us that it's time for a change. The fact is, seasons change and we ought to be spiritually attuned with what God is doing at certain times in our lives, or we could end up languishing in a place that has become dry and unfruitful (case in point, Elijah). An understanding of the different seasons accompanying our Christian walk will reduce needless pain and suffering and improve our enjoyment of the abundant life in Jesus Christ.

Pray with me: Father God, in the name of Jesus, let us be mindful that seasons change and help us to know when our time for change has come.

He's bringing us out

"Many are the afflictions of the righteous: but the Lord delivers him out of them all" (Psalm 34:19).

Child of God, in case you are wondering why your walk with the Lord is being obstructed by so much trouble, scripture tells us that that's the lot of the follower of Christ. The Psalmist in our text tells us that afflictions, persecutions, and detours are a rite of passage for the just. But it doesn't end there. The second part of that verse reassures us that our help is on the way.

The loudest amen, the most "likes" and the highest number of "shares" are usually reserved for any teaching that highlights the glamorous side, the benefits of serving the Lord. However, it's possible to accentuate the positives to the degree that some people mistakenly believe that our walk is always as lovely and pleasant as a bed of roses, continuously being showered with blessings from above. A more balanced view, though, is that the most beautiful rose sits on a branch of thorns. Jesus told His disciples in John 16:33, "I have told you these things, so that in me you may have peace. In this world you will have trouble. But take heart! I have overcome the world." Folks, the truth of the matter is, although our journey is littered with prickly situations and disappointments, our deliverer has won the victory and He's bringing us out.

George A. Young wrote a hymn titled "God Leads Us Along," and the chorus sums up the Christian's journey this way:

"Some through the waters, some through the flood,
Some through the fire, but all through the blood;
Some through great sorrow, but God gives a song,
In the night season and all the day long."

Praise the Lord, in spite of the roadside bombs and other hazards along the battle field, Saints, He's bringing us out.

Let's praise and adore Him!

"Be thankful in all circumstances, for this is God's will for you who belong to Christ Jesus" (1 Thessalonians 5:18).

Let's thank the Lord for the privilege of thanking Him. We ought to get up every day thanking the Lord for the opportunity to say "thanks" because there were many folks who did not make it through the night. It does not matter the situation in which we find ourselves, there is always something for which to say thanks. It's so easy to raise our voice and hands in praise and thanksgiving when we are "on top of the world"—when we have attained our goals and life is good.

What about the not-so-good times? Friend, the word of God says in our text that it is the will of God for us to give thanks in everything. Therefore, when we complain and gripe without thanking the Lord, we are in essence outside of His will. As people of faith, we have no other alternative but to give thanks regardless of the circumstances.

Set Apart

My friends, it's time to set ourselves apart as holy vessels before the Lord. We have wandered and played the harlot (metaphorically) for much too long. It's time to repent and look to our God who provides for His people. He will transfer the wealth of the wicked to a people who worship the King of Kings and the Lord of Lords, the True and Living God, under the banner: *"Set Apart As Holy To The Lord."* Let's pray! Father God, we turn from our waywardness and embrace your grace. Forgive us of our sins and cleanse us from all unrighteousness, in the name of Jesus. Thank you for making us, according to 1 Peter 2:9, "a chosen generation, a royal priesthood, an holy nation, a peculiar people; that we should show forth the praises of him who hath called us out of darkness into his marvelous light." Amen!

References (Isaiah 23:18; Isaiah 60:5–9; Zechariah 14:20, 21; 1 John 1:9; 1 Peter 2:9)

Let's look to God for renewed strength today

Have you not known? Have you not heard? The everlasting God, the LORD, The Creator of the ends of the earth, neither faints nor is weary. His understanding is unsearchable. He gives power to the weak, And to *those who have* no might He increases strength. Even the youths shall faint and be weary, And the young men shall utterly fall, But those who wait on the LORD Shall renew *their* strength; They shall mount up with wings like eagles, They shall run and not be weary, They shall walk and not faint (Isaiah 40:28–31).

Our God reigns

Isaiah 52:7 "How beautiful on the mountains are the feet of those who bring good news, who proclaim peace, who bring good tidings, who proclaim salvation, who say to Zion, "Your God reigns!"

Looking back over yesterday may not bring the most pleasant of memories but here we are today—a new day that the Lord has made. We have new mercies and grace; and a mind to look unto Jesus, the author and finisher of our faith. The Prince of peace is with us today, and He has given us another chance to show the world that He reigns supreme among the nations, kings, and kingdoms. Yes, our God reigns, and we are His ambassadors. Let's give Him praise and glory!

Persevere in Prayer

"And I will wait (call) upon the Lord, that hideth his face from the house of Jacob, and I will look for him" (Isaiah 8:17).

Do you feel like God is hiding His face from you, that He is not hearing your call? Then, be as persistent as the Prophet Isaiah; keep calling and diligently search for Him with your whole heart. Jeremiah 33:3 says "Call upon me, and I will answer thee, and shew thee great and mighty things, which thou knowest not." Keep calling and keep looking!

It's good to serve the Lord

Psalm 84:11 "For the Lord God is a sun and shield: the Lord will give grace and glory: no good thing will he withhold from them that walk uprightly."

The same God who blessed Abraham and promised to be his protector and great reward in Genesis 15:1 is our God. The Lord will leave no stone unturned in His effort to reward all those who serve Him. The text reinforces the point that we who have no other gods are the apple of our Father's eye.

The Lord watches over us because we are the sheep of His pasture, and He is the Good Shepherd. Let's graze with all rights and privileges wherever we happen to be today. Whatever we need He will provide; and "no good thing will he withhold from them who walk uprightly."

It's midnight

"And at midnight Paul and Silas prayed, and sang praises unto God: and the prisoners heard them. And suddenly there was a great earthquake, so that the foundations of the prison were shaken: and immediately all doors were opened, and everyone's bands were loosed" (Acts 16:25–26).

Friends, it's midnight. Let's flood the gates of heaven with our prayers and songs of praise. Let the mighty sound emanating from countless tongues reverberate across land and sea. Let every captive soul hear with expectancy our voices' appeal to our slumberless Deliverer. Suddenly, in the dark of night, the walls of oppression and cruel bondage will be shaken at their core. The merciless shackles that held us in confinement will be broken, and every closed door opened. Hallelujah!

Saints, sing with me, "The Lion of Judah shall break every chain and give us the victory again and again." Give the Lord praise and glory, for he has done great things. He has given us the victory.

If you need a touch from the Lord today, pray with me

Heavenly Father, my fountain of living waters, heal me and I shall be healed; save me, and I shall be saved: for thou art my praise; in the precious name of Jesus. Reference: Jeremiah 17:13–14

Let's drink from the Lord and be filled with His Spirit today.

In the last day, that great day of the feast, Jesus stood and cried, saying, If any man thirst, let him come unto me, and drink. 38 He that believeth on me, as the scripture hath said, out of his belly shall flow rivers of living water. 39 (But this spake he of the Spirit, which they that believe on him should receive: for the Holy Ghost was not yet given; because that Jesus was not yet glorified.)" (John 7:37–39).

I'm reminded of the following chorus:
"Fill my cup Lord; I lift it up, Lord!
Come and quench this thirsting of my soul;

Bread of heaven, Feed me till I want no more—
Fill my cup, fill it up and make me whole!"

Enter into God's quiet rest

Hebrews 4:9–11 says, "So there is a special rest still waiting for the people of God. For all who enter into God's rest will find rest from their labors, just as God rested after creating the world. Let us do our best to enter that place of rest. For anyone who disobeys God, as the people of Israel did, will fall." In 1903, Cleland B. McAfee wrote the words to a hymn titled "There Is a Place of Quiet Rest." I hope the lyrics will help to usher us into a place of rest today:

There is a place of quiet rest,
Near to the heart of God.
A place where sin cannot molest,
Near to the heart of God.

O Jesus, blest Redeemer,
Sent from the heart of God,
Hold us who wait before Thee
Near to the heart of God.

Like King Solomon, we should ask for wisdom

"Give me now wisdom and knowledge that I may go out and come in before this people." (2 Chronicles 1:10).

Friend, we hope that our leaders pray also for wisdom and may the Lord bless them with it. However, as individuals we need the wisdom of God to succeed in our day to day activities, relationships and decision-making. Pray the following prayer with me:

Father God, by your Holy Spirit give us wisdom to execute that which you have placed in our hearts to do, in ways that would bring you glory, honor, and blessing in the precious and magnificent name above every other name, Jesus.

Walk in truth

Beloved, I wish above all things that thou mayest prosper and be in health, even as thy soul prospereth. For I rejoiced greatly, when the brethren came and testified of the truth that is in thee, even as thou walkest in truth. I have no greater joy than to hear that my children walk in truth (3 John 2:2–4).

John's obvious delight in the fact that his "children" were walking in truth led him to pronounce a blessing of health and prosperity upon them. Are we walking in truth today? Are we walking worthy of the vocation for which we were called? Children of the Most High God, if we want to enjoy the rights and privileges of the Kingdom of Heaven, which includes divine prosperity, we too must "walk in truth." Let's pray:

Father God, lead us by your Holy Spirit because you will only direct us into truth, in the name of Jesus Christ.

Lord you are amazing, and I thank you!

"Enter into his gates with thanksgiving, and into his courts with praise: be thankful unto him, and bless his name. For the Lord is good; his mercy is everlasting; and his truth endureth to all generations" (Psalm 100:4–5).

Americans celebrate Thanksgiving Day on the last Thursday in November each year, with much feasting and family fun, and that's good. But how often do we make time in our busy schedule to enter into God's presence with reverence, and heap thanks, praise, and blessings upon Him for the important, little things he does for us each day? Friend, it's good to break for a moment each day and say, "Lord, you are amazing; and I thank you."

Haven't I said that all things are possible? Only believe; the word of God cannot lie.

For as the rain cometh down, and the snow from heaven, and returneth not thither, but watereth the earth, and maketh it bring forth and bud, that it may give seed to the sower, and bread to the eater: [11]So shall my word be that goeth forth out of my mouth: it shall not return unto me void, but it shall accomplish that which I please, and it shall prosper in the thing whereto I sent it (Isaiah 55:10–11).

Every word, every promise, every decree and declaration in the Bible are true. If God said it, you can bet your future earnings on that truth because it will come to pass. The situation may seem impossible with the natural eyes but stand firm, my friend, God's word will do whatever it was sent out to accomplish. Relax, don't work up a sweat over the matter; just take the Lord at His word, trust Him, and you will see the salvation of the Lord.

Only worshipers will receive the rain

"And it shall be, that whoso will not come up of all the families of the earth unto Jerusalem to worship the King, the Lord of hosts, even upon them shall be no rain" (Zechariah 14:17). Some believers think that casting their votes for one candidate over another will bring the blessing upon them. Not so! While it is essential that we exercise our civic duty to vote, it should be understood that "the earth is the Lord's" and that "every good and perfect gift comes from above." More importantly, know that only those who worship the King of

Kings and the Lord of Lords shall enjoy the rain of God's blessing in these times.

Only God has the power to send rain wherever and on whomever he chooses—not our favorite candidate or political party. Amos 4:7 (NLT) states "I kept the rain from falling when you needed it most, ruining all your crops. I sent rain on one town but withheld it from another. Rain fell on one field, while another field withered away." Friend, while we are perfectly justified in carrying out our civic duty by casting our votes according to conscience, remember what the man of God said in Psalm 121:2, "My help comes from the Lord, which made heaven and earth." Child of God, our help comes from God, and only worshipers will receive the rain.

Legitimate reasons to boast

> This is what the LORD says: "Don't let the wise boast in their wisdom, or the powerful boast in their power, or the rich boast in their riches. 24) But those who wish to boast should boast in this alone: that they truly know me and understand that I am the LORD who demonstrates unfailing love and who brings justice and righteousness to the earth and that I delight in these things. I, the LORD, have spoken!" (Jeremiah 9:23–24)

Saints, sometimes when the Lord has shown himself mighty on our behalf, the urge to testify loudly, to brag on Him bubbles up on the inside like a broken fountain filled with hallelujah praises. Those are the days when we can appreciate the Psalmist's pronouncement in Psalm 34:2, "My soul shall make her boast in the LORD: the humble shall hear thereof, and be glad." Some folks may not understand why we are joyful, loud, excited and radical in our praise; so let's take a little time-out to tell of his "loving-kindness, judgment, and righteousness in the earth."

Let the earth reverberate with the sound of God's people bragging boisterously until even the self-restrained will break out of their reservation and testify with gusto. Child of God, according to the text, unlike those who boast about their earthly wisdom, power, and riches, we have legitimate reasons to boast. Go ahead and make your boast in the Lord!

Our deliverance is wrapped up in praise

And when he had consulted with the people, he appointed singers unto the Lord, and that should praise the beauty of holiness, as they went out before the army, and to say, Praise the Lord; for his mercy endureth for ever. 22) And when they began to sing and to praise, the Lord set ambushments against the children of Ammon, Moab, and mount Seir, which were come against Judah; and they were smitten (2 Chronicles 20:21–22).

Often, we wait to see a positive result before we get happy and sing and praise the Lord. But according to our text, God responds to praise in advance of and during our crises. Child of God, we ought to praise the name of our God with a song and magnify Him with thanksgiving (Psalm 69:30).

Let heaven and earth resound, as we praise the beauty of His holiness and His enduring mercy. Praise Him in the morning, in the evening, and at night. Let everything that hath breath praise the Lord (Psalm 150:6). Friend, praise the name of the God of Abraham, Isaac, and Jacob—our God and Father of the Lord and Savior, Jesus Christ! Our deliverance is wrapped up in praise.

Persecution and suffering

In Matthew 5:10, Jesus said, "blessed are they which are persecuted for righteousness sake: for theirs is the kingdom of heaven." Also, we are reminded that "all that will live godly in Christ Jesus shall suffer persecution" (2 Timothy 3:12). Friend, endure with patience; our blessing is already prepared and waiting for us. Don't give up now; victory is ours!

Power to be witnesses

"But ye shall receive power, after that the Holy Ghost is come upon you: and ye shall be witnesses unto me both in Jerusalem, and in all Judaea, and in Samaria, and unto the uttermost part of the earth" (Acts 1:8).

According to our text, the power to witness for Christ comes after the baptism of the Holy Spirit. Acts 8 tells the story about new converts to Christ in Samaria who received the baptism of the Holy Spirit through the laying on of hands by the Apostles including Peter and John. The book of Acts provides us with other instances where converts received the baptism of the Holy Spirit. The story of Cornelius in Acts chapter 10 is a prime example of the Lord pouring out His Spirit upon new converts in a very dramatic way.

> While Peter yet spake these words, the Holy Ghost fell on all them which heard the word. And they of the circumcision which believed were astonished, as many as came with Peter, because that on the Gentiles also was poured out the gift of the Holy Ghost. For they heard them speak with tongues, and magnify God. Then answered Peter, can any man forbid water, that these should not be baptized, which have received the Holy Ghost as well as we? And he commanded them to be baptized in the name of the Lord." (Acts 10:44-48).

The gift of the Holy Spirit provides boldness and the power to be witnesses.

Speak, Lord

"Follow peace with all men, and holiness, without which no man shall see the Lord" (Hebrews 12:14).

Praise the Lord! As much as we would like to be well liked by all, the time has come for the man or woman of God to say what thus says the Lord. Too long we have acquiesced under the pressure to sound like everyone else and say all the "nice" things that would attract attention and favor from the masses. But the Lord is turning us around back to holiness, without which no one shall see God. It is not presumptuous to say that we had gotten complacent, thinking that grace would cover our wanton disregard of God's word; that a little sin here or there did not matter in the larger scheme of things because of the grace of God resident in the blood of Jesus.

It is time for us, the body of Christ to walk in the Spirit; to resist the devil and keep resisting. Jesus showed us the way, giving us his word and sending us the Holy Spirit, as our comforter and resident guide toward truth. Folks, we have no excuse. Right living sets the example for nonbelievers to follow. Talk is cheap. Now, you and I must walk the walk. Lord, help us to walk worthy of the vocation for which we are called, in Jesus' name (Ephesians 4:1).

Preaching Christ crucified may sound foolish to some but ...

"The foolishness of God is wiser than men; and the weakness of God is stronger than men" (1 Corinthians 1:25).

Friend, the power of God and the wisdom of God are available through Jesus Christ who was crucified for our sins. If you would like to know Jesus as Savior and Lord, all you have to do is confess with your mouth that Jesus is Lord and believe in your heart that God raised Him from the dead and you are saved (Romans 10:9). Now, find a Bible-believing church, fellowship with other believers, and study the word of God.

Revive us and our land again, O Lord

Wilt thou not revive us again: that thy people may rejoice in thee? Shew us thy mercy, O LORD, and grant us thy salvation. I will hear what God the LORD will speak: for he will speak peace unto his people, and to his saints: but let them not turn again to folly. Surely his salvation is nigh them that fear him; that glory may dwell in our land. Mercy and truth are met together; righteousness and peace have kissed each other. Truth shall spring out of the earth; and righteousness shall look down from heaven. Yea, the LORD shall give that which is good; and our land shall yield her increase. Righteousness shall go before him; and shall set us in the way of his steps (Psalm 85:6–13).

The people of God are praying and anticipating a revival in the church, across the land and throughout the nations of the earth, but revival must begin in each individual's heart. Child of God, the church is not the building or the place we meet, it's us; and if we expect revival, then every individual must turn away from folly and seek the Lord. The word of the Lord says in 2 Chronicles 7:14 "If my people, which are called by my name, shall humble themselves, and pray, and seek my face, and turn from their wicked ways; then will I hear from heaven, and will forgive their sin, and will heal their land."

Do you want to see the kind of revival mentioned in our text (Psalm 85:6–13)? Then let us examine ourselves and according to Hosea 10:12 "Sow to yourselves in righteousness, reap in mercy; break up your fallow ground: for *it is* time to seek the LORD, till he come and rain righteousness upon you." Revive us and our land again, O Lord! Let's examine ourselves.

Right thinking

Finally, brethren, whatsoever things are true, whatsoever things are honest, whatsoever things are just, whatsoever things are pure, whatsoever things are lovely, whatsoever things are of good report; if there be any virtue, and if there be any praise, think on these things (Philippians 4:8).

Lord, help us to think with the mind of Christ. Grant us the peace that passes all understanding and let our thoughts be edifying, constructive and life-giving. Father God, your word says in Proverbs 23:7 "For as he thinks in his heart, so is he" therefore, we desire to practice right thinking. According to Philippians 4:8, we wish to present a wholesome image of who Jesus is every day. Lord, thank you for enabling us to practice right thinking; in the name of Jesus.

Say Amen

"So Abram departed, as the Lord had spoken unto him" (Genesis 12:4).

I don't know what the Lord has spoken to you, but by faith say amen. Faith in God means obeying His directive even when we don't understand. Note that Abram, the man we now call Abraham did not hesitate; he "departed, as the Lord had spoken unto him." Stop trying to figure it out and say amen to the will of God for your life. Hebrews 11:8 states that "By faith Abraham, when he was called to go out into a place which he should after receive for an inheritance, obeyed; and he went out, not knowing where he was going."

You may feel like father Abraham right now—not knowing how things are going to work out but just say amen, Lord and let faith move you into the promise. Church we have got to learn to say amen to God, regardless of our apprehensions because faith in God is not about how we feel; it's about pleasing God (Hebrews 11:6). Are you willing to follow God today, where ever He may lead? I like the lyrics to an Andre Crouch song, "Let the Church Say Amen":

"Let the church say amen, let the church say amen
God has spoken, so let the church say amen
Let the church, let 'em say amen
If you believe the word, let the whole church say amen"

Child of God, as we travel on this journey of faith today, let's say amen to the word of God and step out by faith. James 2:23–24 declares in part "Abraham believed God, and it was accounted to him for righteousness." And he was called the friend of God. You see then that a man is justified by works, and not by faith only." Amen!

Lord, by Your Spirit, shine through us today

"Let your light so shine before men, that they may see your good works, and glorify your Father which is in heaven." (Matthew 5:16).

I'm reminded of a quote suggesting that if one was not a part of the solution then one was in fact, a part of the problem. As children of God, we are supposed to be the ones with the solutions to the world's problems—light in a dark world. We have been designated the beneficiaries, custodians, and shining examples of "Christ in me, the hope of glory." Are we living up to our mandate by reflecting the righteousness and true holiness of our Lord and Savior, Jesus Christ? Do our actions influence the folks around us to the degree that they yearn for a personal relationship with the Christ in us?

In a message titled: "Colossians 1:27—Christ in you, the hope of glory," Wil Pounds (2007) said "Christ in you is glory. In having Christ, you have glory. Christ's glory and your glory are wrapped up together. If Christ were to lose you, it would be a great loss to Him. If I can perish with Christ in me He will lose His honor. His glory is gone if one soul who has put their trust in Him for eternal life is ever cast away. As sure as the Lord God lives, Christ in you means you in glory with Him for all eternity. This is the most astounding truth taught in the Bible. "Christ in you."

If we have this truth in us, Christ, the only hope for eternity then His glory should be reflected on whom ever we meet, where ever we go. Our message should be unrelenting, our love undying, our peace unperturbed, and our actions beyond reproach. Government leaders should be requesting our audience and our prayers sought after by private and business sectors. Let's bring glory to our Father in heaven. Pray with me:

Lord, by Your Spirit, shine through us today, in the name of Jesus.

Speaking and hearing as the learned

Wouldn't it be awesome to wake up each day knowing the right thing to say at the appropriate moment and be able to hear with perfect understanding every word spoken to us? Well, according to the word of God, that's the mark of a learned person, one who is plugged into the Spirit of God and is not rebellious. Isaiah 50:4 states, "The Lord God has given me the tongue of the learned, that I should know how to speak a word in season to him that is weary; he wakeneth morning by morning, he wakeneth mine ear to hear as the learned." The next verse implies that we fail to apply what we have heard because of rebellion. Let's strive to speak and hear as the learned on a daily basis.

Strength and peace

"The Lord will give strength unto his people; the Lord will bless his people with peace." (Psalm 29:11).

Strength: According to Nehemiah 8:10, the joy of the Lord is our strength; and Psalm 16:11 tells us that in the presence of God there is fullness of joy. It follows then that our strength comes from spending time in the presence of God. Conversely, the less time spent praying, reading, and meditating on God's word, the weaker we get (spiritually) and thus, the easier it becomes to buckle under the pressures of life.

Peace: Isaiah 26:3 states that we get perfect peace by keeping our minds stayed on God. Saints, peace is a blessing from the Lord and we can only experience this fruit of the Spirit by putting God first in our lives, becoming "God intoxicated." The peace of God makes it possible to rest comfortably in the midst of a raging financial turmoil besieging financial markets on Wall Street and around the world. Also, God's peace restrains the child of God in a climate of hostile, negative campaigning being unleashed on a fragile and frightened electorate.

Friend, in these troubled times we need strength and peace. But these two rewards are dependent on our relationship with the Lord. We must spend time seeking God and sacrificing our time in His presence. There, we will find the joy that gives us the strength we need to endure (Psalm 16:11). Finally, the blessing of peace is perhaps the most sought after commodity in life. The rich will tell you that money and riches do not bring lasting peace. Celebrity status does not guarantee peace. Ask some of our most famous rock stars, artists, and movie stars. Peace will remain an illusion to those who have rejected the Lord Jesus Christ and have not been born again. Let's pray:

Lord, we are your people; give us strength and bless us with peace today, in the name of Jesus.

Take time to know the Lord

My Father has given me authority over everything. No one really knows the Son except the Father, and no one really knows the Father except the Son and those to whom the Son chooses to reveal him. Take my Yoke upon you. Let me teach you, because I am humble and gentle, and you will find rest for your souls (Matthew 11:27–29, NLT).

Rational minds would agree that it takes time for two individuals to build a right relationship; that is, to reach and maintain the highest levels of intimacy with each other. It takes time to get to that point where they are able to finish each other's sentences, where a smile carries a much deeper meaning to the two than anyone around them could ever imagine, and the desire for each other burns with a passion that goes beyond fleshly self-gratification. At this place of knowing, both lovers understand the ways, likes, dislikes, and the little idiosyncrasies of their spouse.

Similarly, developing a deeper relationship with Christ takes time; knowing Him and "the power of His resurrection" is based on a relationship, which is a building process. Jesus said in our text that no one knows Him (the Son) but His Father and that no one knows the Father except the Son. But here is the clincher at the end of verse 27, "and those whom the Son chooses to reveal Him." Child of God, only Jesus can reveal the Father to us, and if you take a look at verse 29 you will see that Jesus wants us to learn about Him. He wants us to spend time with Him to know of His humility and gentleness and to find rest in His presence.

Are you willing to take the time to know the Lord; to develop a fulfilling and everlasting relationship that provides an easy yoke and a lighter burden? Do you want to glow with love, peace, joy, humility, and the other attributes of the fruit of the Spirit of God? One can only reach that level of intimacy with God through Jesus Christ, by spending quality time getting to know Him. A popular song some years ago told the story of a young man who went to his mother with the news that he desired to marry a certain girl. The mother responded with these words: "Take time to know her; love is not an overnight thing."

It is the will of God that we get to know Him; that we take the time to learn His waysand grow to love Him so that we may reflect His true image. Friend, take time to know the Lord; become a seeker and a "God chaser." Resolve to spend quality time getting to know the Lord.

Thank God for the Blood of Jesus

"LORD, if you kept a record of our sins, who, O Lord could ever survive? 4) But you offer forgiveness that we might learn to fear (reverence) you" (Psalm 130:3–4).

The Psalmist in our text sang of a loving gracious God who does not keep a record of all our wrong deeds because if He did, none of us would be alive today. But the Lord forgives us, so that we might be grateful enough to reverence Him. In Psalm 143:2, the word of God again declares that no man living is justified in the eyes of God. The good news is that Father God has made a way through which we can be justified, that is, to be in right standing before Him.

That's the reason for celebrating Easter, a time when we mark with gratitude, the death, burial, and resurrection of the Lord Jesus, the Lamb who takes away the sin of the world.

Friend, the Blood of the Jesus now gives us legitimacy; our hearts can truly rejoice that God does not keep a record of the wrongs we've done; that instead He has made a way for us to be justified before Him. Our God, in His infinite love toward us has provided a mediator between Himself and man, the Lord Jesus Christ by whose Blood we are considered righteous, without a guilty stain (see John 3:16–17).

If anyone reading this book does not know this Jesus by whose Blood we are cleansed and made righteous before God, simply confess with your mouth that Jesus is Lord and believe in your heart that God raised Him from the dead and that you are saved (see Romans 10:9–10). Child of God, let's thank God for the Blood of Jesus. "What can wash away my sins? Nothing but the blood of Jesus. What can make me whole again? Nothing but the blood of Jesus"

Thank the Lord for His word

"Your word is a lamp for my feet and a light for my path" (Psalm 119:105, NLT).

A few years ago I spent time in a pristinely beautiful, mountainous region of Jamaica. Part of the attractiveness of this region is the absence of some of the modern conveniences that some folks in first world nations take for granted, including electricity. To the uninitiated, nighttime poses some challenges, most noteworthy of which is walking from point A to point B in thick, blinding darkness, as scary as the night in a horror movie. Therefore, anyone who was brave enough to venture out after dark has to use a lamp or lantern.

Child of God, as we traverse the path of life with its spiritual blind spots and unlit highways and byways— the result of sin and wickedness—we need light. The Psalmist is saying in our text that the word of God is able to shine onto our pathway, making our walk in the dark easier and less risky. Let's thank the Lord for His word that guides our steps today.

Thank the Lord for mercy!

For the Lord hath called thee as a woman forsaken and grieved in spirit, and a wife of youth, when thou wast refused, saith thy God. 7) For a small moment have I forsaken thee, but with great mercies will I gather thee. 8) In a little wrath I hid my face from thee for a moment, but with everlasting kindness will I have mercy on thee, saith the Lord thy redeemer (Isaiah 54:6–8).

Friend, from the depths of our hearts let's thank the Lord for His mercy. But, you say, my condition is miserable; it is dark and my life seems to be going nowhere. Child of God, thank Him still. I can remember over forty years ago, being lost, defeated, and confused, and feeling as if my young life was over in the land of my birth. I had failed to live up to the expectations of teachers, family, friends, and the church. I felt ashamed and for years wondered if God would ever restore me to a place of success and prosperity.

But, thanks be to God for His word; this text in the book of Isaiah for reasons I did not know then became a source of comfort and hope. I found tranquility even for a moment at a time in this powerful promise of God to His people Israel. It made me feel like a fussy child might feel with a pacifier pressed gently against the tongue into a waiting mouth. As a result, even in my less than ideal condition at the time, I would hold on to God's promise of mercy and restoration. Suffice it to say that the Lord, over time, has turned my mourning, sadness, marginalization, and hopelessness into a time of rejoicing and dancing—a time of thanksgiving.

The lesson here, my travailing friend, is that it's not over yet. You are loved and the grace and mercy of God will bring you deliverance. Hold on to the promises of the God of Isaiah, the God of our Lord and Savior Jesus Christ. Young person, you are not alone; you are on God's mind. Yes, it may be dark and seemingly hopeless, but the God of Israel will intervene. Remember, "Weeping may endure for a night but joy comes in the morning" (Psalm 30:5).

Thank you Lord

"O give thanks unto the Lord; for he is good; for his mercy endureth for ever" (1 Chronicles 16:34).

Father God, with grateful hearts we exalt Your holy name. Thank You for being our God. For goodness and mercy, we are compelled to "give thanks unto the Lord." For salvation paid for by the shed blood of Jesus Christ and allocated to us by grace through faith, thank You, Lord. For such incomprehensible, fathomless love, we have no other option but to thank You, Lord.

Abba, for the air we breathe and the food we eat, thank You. For clothing, shelter and divine protection, thank You, Lord. For family, friends and the people You have appointed to help us on our journey, thank You. For wisdom, understanding and a mind to serve You, thank You, Lord.

Your word admonishes us in 1 Thessalonians 5:18 to give thanks in every situation. Therefore, we will be mindful to always thank You. Whether in laughter or through tears, we will remember to thank You Lord; in the precious name of Jesus.

Thanks and praise

For another day to give you glory, honor and praise
For grace, mercy and unfailing love, even though we are undeserving
For your Holy Spirit who draws all people to you
For the preaching of the gospel of Jesus Christ
For faith to dream and do the impossible

For loving family and friends
For the smile or kind word from a stranger that changed the drab colors, brightened our mood and gave us reason to hope again
For those who sent us running to you by making our lives difficult and unbearable
For being our present help in time of trouble
For peace in the midst of the storms of life
For strength made perfect in weakness
For food, clothing and shelter
Father, for everything we give you thanks
In the name of Jesus!

Friend, everyone has something for which to thank the Lord. One writer wrote "When I think of the goodness of the Lord and all that He has done for me, my soul cries hallelujah." We must give God thanks, unless one does not believe that there is a God, which would be a tragedy because Psalm 53:1 states "The fool hath said in his heart, "There is no God." Child of God, let's thank the Lord God Almighty.

The danger has passed and your deliverance is here

Psalm 34:7 "The angel of the Lord encampeth round about them that fear him, and delivereth them."

The Lord has delivered you from all harm and danger. His anointing is upon you. The eye of your understanding is now open to discern that thing. Unruly spirits must bow to the name of Jesus. Every ungodly element has been destroyed by the fire of the Holy Spirit and you are now free. Praise the name of the Lord, the Holy One of Israel, in Jesus' name.

The Lord hears only the righteous

"For the eyes of the Lord are over the righteous, and his ears are open unto their prayers: but the face of the Lord is against them that do evil" (1 Peter 3:12).

I like what the man who received his sight said to the Pharisees in John 10:31: "Now we know that God heareth not sinners: but if any man be a worshipper of God, and doeth his will, him he heareth." Let's forsake evil, so that our prayers may be answered. Our God is holy and will not reside among the wicked.

The Lord is always near when we need Him.

"When my father and my mother forsake me, then the Lord will take me up" (Psalm 27:10).

To all those who woke up this morning devastated by circumstances, be encouraged. You are not forsaken. If you feel like there is nowhere to go and no one to turn to, remember that you are not alone. God is with you. Though your temporal world may have crumbled and you are left with less than the bare essentials, help is on the way—Jehovah Jireh will provide for you.

The Lord is our shelter from the storm, a father to the fatherless, and our help in time of trouble. Hope in God. He will never leave us nor forsake us, even when we feel like no one is there for us in the natural. The Lord promises to give us the direction and guidance we need to navigate our course through life's journey. In Psalm 32:8, the word states "I will instruct thee and teach thee in the way which thou shalt go: I will guide thee with mine eye." Friend, all we need to do is trust and obey God. The Lord is always near when we need Him. Glory to His name!

Let's give God the glory that's rightfully His

Daniel 4:3 "How great are his signs! And how mighty are his wonders! His kingdom is an everlasting kingdom, and his dominion is from generation to generation."

Twenty five centuries ago, there was a great Babylonian ruler named Nebuchadnezzar (of Shadrach, Meshach, and Abednego fame) who had allowed pride to transform his humanness into an illusionary image of deity. Unfortunately for him, God had already stated emphatically that He would not share His glory with anyone. The text is an indication that Nebuchadnezzar's delusion of grandeur was short-lived and eventually he had to bow his knees and confess the awesomeness of our God.

The same is true for many of us today, as we have in large part become self-absorbed, self-sufficient, and have in many respects excluded God from our lives. Some folks have forgotten that they need a Savior and that His praise should continually flow from their mouths. Remember, regardless of the power we wield and the vast scope of our influence, in our respective domains, every one of us at some point in time will have to humble ourselves under the mighty hand of God and acknowledge that Jesus Christ is Lord. The Apostle Paul warns in Philippians 2:10 that "Every knee shall bow and every tongue shall confess that Jesus Christ is Lord."

Friend, if anything or anyone has taken the place of God in your life, it would be safe to assume that your life is not glorifying our Creator. Nebuchadnezzar found out that pride and self-glorification led only to destruction and that mankind was ultimately created to praise the one true God. What about you? Please bow your knees, while there is still time and ask Jesus Christ to take center stage and be Lord of your life. God desires his rightful place on the throne of our hearts. Then and only then will we be able to proclaim His glory.

For those who do not know the King of Glory and would like to make Him Savior and Lord, please pray with me:

I confess that Jesus is my Lord and I believe that God has raised Him (Jesus) from the dead. I am saved by God's grace. Thank you Lord (Romans 10:9–10). Now, let's give God the glory that's rightfully His.

The Lord will never disappoint those who trust Him

"Yet you are holy. The praises of Israel surround your throne. Our ancestors trusted in you, and you rescued them. You heard their cries for help and saved them. They put their trust in you and were never disappointed" (Psalm 22:3–5).

Child of God, keep trusting; don't give up now. Everything will be all right, in Jesus' name. Daniel was saved from the lions. Shadrach, Meshach, and Abednego were rescued by the fourth man in the fiery furnace. Jesus was raised from the dead and now holds all power. Friend, the end of the story says that we are the winners. Don't give up now; trust God and He will never disappoint you.

The word of God will sustain us

"Thy word have I hid in mine heart, that I might not sin against thee" (Psalm 119:11).

The greatest antidote for the lure of sin and unrighteous thoughts is the word of God. The battle for our souls is fought largely in the mind; therefore, the Lord has given us a foolproof, guaranteed method for overcoming any ungodly inclination. Child of God, the word cleanses the mind and purifies our thoughts.

The Psalmist declares in Psalm 1:2 that our delight should be in the word of God and that we should meditate on it day and night. Psalm 119:11 sums up this time-tested way of living above the attraction of sin, which is by keeping or hiding God's word in our hearts. Friend, this is the only sure way of minimizing the ungodly urges that trouble every one of us, especially at our weakest moments.

A day is coming when God shall reign in our favor forever

Micah 4:7 declares "And I will make her that halted a remnant, and her that was cast off a strong nation: and the Lord shall reign over them in mount Zion from henceforth, even forever."

Many lives have been shipwrecked because of the unwise and myopic rule of heathen leaders; however, God is about to put the pieces back together. The Lord will intervene, showing Himself to be mighty among the nations; and will reign eternally to the delight of all His children. Hallelujah to the Lamb!

Some Bible scholars will make valid arguments that our text refers specifically to Israel and that may be true. But Child of God, Revelation 11:15 states, "And the seventh angel sounded; and there were great voices in heaven, saying, the kingdoms of this world are become the kingdoms of our Lord, and of his Christ; and he shall reign for ever and ever." There is one thing we can be sure of friends; a day is coming when God shall reign in our favor forever. Remain encouraged and stay optimistic.

There is a ram in the bush for somebody; your Jehovah-Jireh has provided.

And Abraham lifted up his eyes, and looked, and behold behind him a ram caught in the thicket by his horns: and Abraham went and took the ram, and offered him up for a burnt offering in the stead of his son. And Abraham called the name of the place

Jehovah-Jireh: as it is said to this day, in the mount of the Lord it shall be seen (Genesis 22:13, 14).

Although the situation had seemed critical, yet in the eleventh hour the Lord had provided. Bless His holy name! It's possibly your eleventh hour, and you are concerned about the rent that's due, the tuition payment that's approaching at the start of the new semester, or maybe the doctor's report that painted a picture of sadness, causing serious bout of anxiety. Not to worry, child of God, listen carefully; there is the bleating of a ram just around the corner. Your Jehovah Jireh has imposed His sovereignty, defying the principles of natural law. God is about to make what had seemed impossible possible.

There is power in prayer

Are any among you sick? They should call for the elders of the church and have them pray over them, anointing them with oil in the name of the Lord. 15) And the prayer offered in faith will heal the sick, and the Lord will make them well. And anyone who has committed sins will be forgiven. 16) Confess your sins to each other and pray for each other so that you may be healed. The earnest prayer of a righteous person has great power and wonderful results. 17) Elijah was as human as we are, and yet when he prayed earnestly that no rain would fall, none fell for the next three and a half years! 18) Then he prayed for rain, and down it poured. The grass turned green, and the crops began to grow again" (James 5:14–18, NLT).

Jesus made it perfectly clear that the church should be a place of prayer rather than a marketplace for profit. Prayer is a potent weapon to be used unceasingly by every believer and the church in general. Have you ever wondered why Jesus always spent time in prayer? The Lord knew that his power came from the Father and that staying connected was the way to stay connected to His source. James 5:16 states in part, "... the earnest prayer of a righteous person has great power and wonderful results."

What do you need from God today? Are you bound by sickness and disease, or troubled by sin? The text advises believers to call for the elders of the church to pray over them and anoint them with oil in the name of Jesus. Your case may seem difficult but it's no match for the power of prayer. Jeremiah 33:3 invites us to call upon God because He answers when we call and will do great and mighty things on our behalf.

The efficacy of prayer was evidenced when the Lord approved Elijah's request that there be no rain for three and a half years. Miracles take place when the righteous pray. Jesus prayed over two fish and five loaves and multiplication took place, leading to the feeding of five thousand people. Friend, there is power in prayer.

Time to leave those idols behind and get fired up for God

"Israel treated it all so lightly—she thought nothing of committing adultery by worshipping idols made of wood and stone. So now the land has been greatly defiled" (Jeremiah 3:9, NLT).

Although Jeremiah was speaking specifically to Israel's retreat from the things of God into idolatry, the text highlights prophetically, the condition of a large segment of the body of Christ today. In New Testament scripture, the church is referred to as the Bride of Christ; who like the virtuous bride, is expected to be clean and pure in anticipation of the return of the bridegroom. Sadly, many of us have strayed from our first love, "committing adultery by worshipping idols." An idol is anything that takes first place in our lives and robs God of our attention, time, true worship, and adoration. How do we get rid of our defilement and become the virtuous Bride again; the light and salt in a world filled with distractions bent on wooing us away from the Lord?

Well, the process begins with the acknowledgment that we need to say no to our spiritual adversary and the sin which so easily besets us. Hebrews 12:1 declares "Therefore; since we are surrounded by such a huge crowd of witnesses to the life of faith, let us strip off every weight that slows us down, especially the sin that so easily trips us up. And let us run with endurance the race God has set before us." Please understand that stripping those weights and resisting such powerful ungodly attractions are futile efforts, if one is armed only with willpower. We need Holy Ghost power, and James 4:7 states, "Submit yourselves therefore to God. Resist the devil, and he will flee from you." Note that one must first submit or surrender one's will unto God in order to receive the power necessary to say no.

Child of God, we must cultivate an intimate relationship with the Lord, by whose Spirit we are able to turn our backs on the things and habits that lead us into religious idolatry. The Prophet Jeremiah relayed a time-tested truth to Israel that is still valid for us today, when he said in Jeremiah 3:13–15 that the idolater should: recognize that he or she is in a sinful state, repent, get back into the word, and grow in the knowledge and understanding of the Lord. The Apostle John sums up the matter without mincing words in 1 John 1:8–9, "If we say we have no sin, we are only fooling ourselves and refusing to accept the truth. But if we confess our sins to him, he is faithful and just to forgive us and to cleanse us from every wrong."

Today is the day of salvation

We must prepare now for what comes after we die because there is no repentance after the grave. Hebrews 9:27–28 (KJV) states "And as it is appointed unto men once to die, but after this the judgment: So Christ was once offered to bear the sins of many; and unto them that look for him shall he appear the second time without sin unto salvation."

The same verse in the NIV says, "Just as people are destined to die once, and after that to face judgment, so Christ was sacrificed once to take away the sins of many; and he will appear a second time, not to bear sin, but to bring salvation to those who are waiting for him."

If anyone does not know Jesus, receive the free gift of salvation today; call upon Him while there is still time. Second Corinthians 6:2 declares "For God says, "At just the right time, I heard you. On the day of salvation, I helped you." Indeed, the "right time" is now. Today is the day of salvation."

Trust God and He will deliver

"In thee, O Lord, do I put my trust; let me never be ashamed: deliver me in thy righteousness" (Psalm 31:1).

Friend, though the circumstance may seem dire, God has a way of turning things around for our benefit. Don't fret or worry; trust Abba (Father) and he will bring you out. Let's pray. Father, we thank you for intervening on our behalf today. We believe that you will "Deliver us from evil; for thine is the kingdom, the power and the glory"—in the name of Jesus; Amen!

Get rid of that prideful spirit now!

"But when his heart was lifted up, and his mind hardened in pride, he was deposed from his kingly throne, and they took his glory from him" (Daniel 5:20). There is writing on the wall. Please don't blame the messenger.

When we think that we are the "captains of our own ships," that we have arrived at a place in life where the need for God is no longer our primary concern, we have surrendered to our own demise. At the onset, let me state emphatically that there is nothing wrong with striving to better oneself and becoming "all you can be." However, if you have reached that exalted place of self-sufficiency in your mind, deluded by personal achievements and the trappings of success, it may be time to check the pride meter.

Satan fell from heaven because of pride (Isaiah 14:12); Nebuchadnezzar tried to make himself a god but instead lost his mind and his kingdom for seven years, as he wandered through the forest like a wild animal (Daniel 4). Belshazzar, his great grandson "lifted up" himself against the Lord of heaven and was assassinated (Daniel 5). Child of God, humility prepares the heart to receive God's riches and promotion in the kingdom of God (James 4:10). The text, although referring specifically to Nebuchadnezzar, paints a graphic image of the dire repercussions of a life of pride. Solomon states that "pride goes before destruction, a haughty spirit before a fall."

If you have been caught up in a spirit that has caused you to minimize the importance of God in your life and have downplayed the significance of those whom He has strategically placed in your life to help you along the way, such as family, friends, and mentors, you are walking on the proverbial slippery slope. Consider this a warning. Get rid of that prideful spirit now!

We are free

"And ye shall know the truth, and the truth shall make you free" (John 8:32).

According to Wesley's notes, "The truth—written in your hearts by the Spirit of God, shall make you free—from guilt, sin, misery, Satan." John 8:36 states "So if the Son sets you free, you are truly free." Aren't you thankful? Let's praise the Lord—we are free!

We are made new in Christ

2 Corinthians 5:17, "Therefore if any man be in Christ, he is a new creature: old things are passed away; behold, all things are become new."

In the name of Jesus, Son of the Living God I decree and declare that you are loosed from the bondage that has held you bound for years. No more, says the Lord; my blood was shed for you, that you be set free. Now, every chain has been broken, every sin that so easily had beset you shall be a thing of the past. You have been resurrected with me says the Lord and have been made new because the same Spirit that raised Jesus from the dead is the same Spirit that quickens your mortal body. You are alive in Jesus today. Arise and flourish as children of light. Your darkness has been made obscure with the light of your Savior's love.

Praise the Lord, we are not forgotten

Child of God, our heavenly Father loves us and will never abandon us, no matter what the situation looks like in the natural. Elevate your faith and trust our awesome God who spoke to the Israelites in Isaiah 49:15–16: "Can a mother forget the baby at her breast and have no compassion on the child she has borne? Though she may forget, I will not forget you! See, I have engraved you on the palms of my hands; your walls are ever before me."

Glory to God! We are always in His memory. So, dry up your tears, Saints, square your shoulders and look up;

redemption is closer than you think. Praise the Lord! We are not forgotten.

We are priests of God; let's wear our mantle well

"Now if you will obey me and keep my covenant, you will be my own special treasure from among all the nations of the earth; for all the earth belongs to me" (Exodus 19:5–6, NLT).

Under the Law of Moses, the priestly order was established to provide spiritual representatives or points of contact between God and man. Today, anyone who has accepted Jesus Christ, "who listens to God's word or obeys it," not only escapes the fate of the disobedient but has been chosen to be priests of God. The Apostle Peter states in 1 Peter 2:5: "And now God is building you, as living stones, into his spiritual temple. What's more, you are God's holy priests, who offer the spiritual sacrifices that please him because of Jesus Christ." Also, 1 Peter 2:9 records, "... for you are a chosen people. You are a kingdom of priests, God's holy nation, and his very own possession. This is so you can show others the goodness of God, for he called you out of darkness into his wonderful light."

Child of God, recognize that we are especially chosen to be God's representatives to declare the goodness of God among our families and neighbors, in the market place of ideas, and among the nations. We ought to live in obedience to the word of God, exemplifying the unique kingdom lifestyle commensurate with our calling. We are beacons of hope in a dark, failing world; pointing the lost to the only Savior of the world, Jesus Christ. We are priests of God; let's wear our mantle well

We are standing on a sure foundation

"The Lord is king! He is robed in majesty. Indeed, the Lord is robed in majesty and armed with strength. The world is firmly established; it cannot be shaken. Your throne, O Lord, has been established from time immemorial. You yourself are from the everlasting past" (Psalm 93:1–2, NLT).

Recent events may have shaken the faith of some folks, but we who are rooted and grounded in Christ understand that our God is still sovereign. We know that Jesus Christ reigns supreme in spite of Satan's attempts to shake the world with a barrage of horrific circumstances meant to destabilize the very foundation of our faith. But today, my friends, let's arise with renewed focus and adore our exalted King, who sits in everlasting dominion on the highest throne. We will not be moved because we are standing on a sure foundation.

We can do it

"For I can do everything with the help of Christ who gives me the strength I need" (Philippians 4:13, NLT). We will not limit ourselves today!
Let's face each circumstance, or challenge with the confidence that success is the only option. The Lord will provide the courage and wherewithal to accomplish whatever exploits we aim to perform in His name. Friends, we can do it—with the help of Christ.

We have been given spiritual gifts by the Holy Spirit

At the onset, know that no one operating by the Spirit of God can curse Jesus, and no one is able to say, "Jesus is Lord," except by the Holy Spirit (1 Corinthians 12:3). Be aware also, that there are different spiritual gifts given by the same Holy Spirit. There are different kinds of service in the church, but we are serving the same Lord. Note that God works in different ways in our lives but it is the same God working in and through us. Spiritual gifts are given to us as a means of helping the entire church (1 Corinthians 12:4–7).

Here are the nine spiritual gifts discussed in 1 Corinthians 12:8–10:

> To one person is given the ability to give advice; to another he gives the gift of special knowledge. The Spirit gives special faith to another, and to someone else he gives the power to heal the sick. He gives one person the power to perform miracles, and to another the ability to prophesy. He gives someone else the ability to know whether it is really the spirit of God or another spirit that is speaking. Still another person is given the ability to speak in unknown languages, and another is given the ability to interpret what is being said.

Note also, that "It is the one and only Holy Spirit who distributes these gifts. He alone decides which gift each person should have (1 Corinthians 12:11). Have you recognized your gifts, and if so, have you been operating accordingly in the church? If not, why?

We need to change because God does not

"I am the Lord, and I do not change" (Malachi 3:6).

If we desire to eat the good of the land and enjoy the abundant life in Christ, we need to change. Yes, we need to exchange our will for His will and live in obedience to His word (Isaiah 1:19). Note that God by His very nature cannot change; neither will He amend his word to accommodate us.

Child of God, we can rest assured that God's love for us has not changed and will never subside, based on the record of His goodness toward us since creation. We can equally be certain that God will not change His position on sin; neither will He alter His offer of salvation to whosoever calls upon the name of the Lord (Romans 10:13). We have a sure path to a victorious life through Jesus Christ, who is the same yesterday, today and forever (Hebrews 13:8). Our unchanging God, in his infinite wisdom and providence, has promised divine prosperity to those who keep His word in their hearts and walk in His way (Joshua 1:8).

The Psalmist declares in Psalm1:3 that all who walk in righteousness will be "like trees planted along the river bank, bearing fruit each season without fail. Their leaves never wither, and in all they do, they prosper." Saint, the God who spoke in the Old Testament is the same God who is instructing us in the New Testament, and 1 Peter 1:26 states "the word of the Lord endureth for ever." It's important that we align our ways with the word of God, which will not only bring glory to Christ but also attract the blessing upon our lives. Remember, we need to change because God does not.

We need right living in the church, even under grace

Titus 2:11–15 (NLT) declares:

For the grace of God has been revealed, bringing salvation to all people. And we are instructed to turn from godless living and sinful pleasures. We should live in this evil world with self-control, right conduct, and devotion to God, while we look forward to that wonderful event when the glory of our great God and Savior, Jesus Christ, will be revealed. He gave his life to free us from every kind of sin, to cleanse us, and to make us his very own people, totally committed to doing what is right. You must teach these things and encourage your people to do them, correcting them when necessary. You have the authority to do this, so don't let anyone ignore you or disregard what you say.

Grace has now become a scapegoat for some folks who believe that sin no longer exists under the new covenant. They imply that the blood of Jesus somehow, makes us immune to sin. They bark at the idea of anyone having to repent of sins because they say that God's grace precludes the need to repent. Some even go as far as to say that any reference to holiness is a step back into bondage (Egypt). I beg to differ. If and when we commit an act which violates God's holy standards, we need to repent and access the grace needed to prevent future violations. This passage in Titus 2 should become mandatory reading for the misinformed on the subject of grace. Thank God for grace!

Welcome His presence

"Whither shall I go from thy spirit? Or whither shall I flee from thy presence?" (Psalm 139:7)
Child of God, this verse should bring us comfort, knowing that we serve a God who is always near. That's exciting news because in the presence of the Lord we have fullness of joy. Nehemiah 8:10 says that the joy of the Lord is our strength. Welcome His presence today

What do you see?

And when the servant of the man of God was risen early, and gone forth, behold, an host compassed the city both with horses and chariots. And his servant said unto him, Alas, my master! how shall we do? 16) And he answered, fear not: for they that be with us are more than they that be with them. 17) And Elisha prayed, and said, Lord, I pray thee, open his eyes, that he may see. And the Lord opened the eyes of the young man; and he saw: and behold, the mountain was full of horses and chariots of fire round about Elisha (2 Kings 6:15–17).

Hallelujah! Friend, back to the question—what do you see? Do you see only the fierce competitor, adversary, or situation so hideous that you have allowed fear to grip your very soul? Do you see an empty wallet, bank account, the pink slip, and an economy gone south? Well, whatever you are seeing, the thing that has been causing you to lose sleep and worry is no match for what's taking place in the realm of the Spirit. But to see the awesome power of God's spiritual might and deliverance taking place around you requires a new vision. People of God we must ask the Lord to open our spiritual eyes of faith so that we may see His reality.

The reality is that our help is here; God is with us. We shall prosper and be in health even as our soul prospers. The enemy is defeated and God is exalted. We are blessed going out and coming in, blessed in the fields, in the city, on the job, and in our businesses. We have a Shepherd that feeds his flock. What do you see? Are you seeing God's possibilities, His promise to supply all our needs according to His riches in glory? Do you see the enemy fleeing when no one chases after him? Man of God and woman of God, we are safe and secure in the arms of the Lord. Let's pray:

Father God, open our spiritual eyes that we may see, in the name of Jesus. Amen!

The oracles of God

We are the temple of the ever-living God; whatever one says ought to represent Him. Some time ago, in one of my postings, I asked the Lord to help me speak as the "oracles of God," and a few friends were offended. As a result, the Holy Spirit prompted me to address the issue with three translations of 1 Peter 4:11 and Colossians 3:17. My prayer is that the Holy Spirit would enlightenment us on this subject. Here are the KJV, NLT, and NIV versions of the two aforementioned verses:

1 Peter 4:11

(KJV) "If any man speaks, let him speak as the oracles of God; if any man ministers, let him do it as of the ability which God gives: that God in all things may be glorified through Jesus Christ, to whom be praise and dominion forever and ever. Amen."

(NLT) "Do you have the gift of speaking? Then speak as though God himself were speaking through you. Do you have the gift of helping others? Do it with all the strength and energy that God supplies. Then everything you do will bring glory to God through Jesus Christ. All glory and power to him forever and ever! Amen."

(NIV) "If anyone speaks, they should do so as one who speaks the very words of God. If anyone serves, they should do so with the strength God provides, so that in all things God may be praised through Jesus Christ. To him be the glory and the power for ever and ever. Amen."

Colossians 3:17

(KJV) "And whatsoever you do in word or deed, do all in the name of the Lord Jesus, giving thanks to God the Father by him.

(NLT) "And whatever you do or say, do it as a representative of the Lord Jesus, giving thanks through him to God the Father.

(NIV) "And whatever you do, whether in word or deed, do it all in the name of the Lord Jesus, giving thanks to God the Father through him."

Your situation only needs a word from God

"By the word of the Lord were the heavens made; and all the host of them by the breath of his mouth. For he spake, and it was done; he commanded, and it stood fast" (Psalm 33:6–9).

Friend, the Almighty God spoke this universe into existence. Think about that for a moment. All He said was "Let there be" and nothing became something. That's the God we serve. Trust Him with every fiber of your being; speak His word over your situation or circumstance and watch God do the impossible in your life. Jeremiah 32:17 proclaims, "Ah Lord God! behold, thou hast made the heaven and the earth by thy great power and stretched out arm, and there is nothing too hard for thee:" Your situation only needs a word from God.

Benediction and blessing

"May the words of my mouth, and the meditation of my heart, be acceptable in thy sight, O Lord, my strength and my redeemer" (Psalm 19:14).

"May the Lord bless you and keep you. May the Lord make his face to shine upon you, and be gracious to you. May the Lord lift up his countenance upon you, and give you peace" (Numbers 6:24–26).

Go now and enjoy victory through surrender!

REFERENCES

McCloud, S. (2011). Maslow's Hierarchy of needs. SimplyPsychology, from http://www.simplypsychology.org/maslow.html

Pounds, W. (2007). Colossians 1:27 "Christ in you, the hope of glory" from http://www.abideinchrist.com/message/col1v27.ht

The Holy Bible, International Standard Version (ISV) © 2012

The Holy Bible, New International Version (NIV) © 2011

The Holy Bible, New Living Translation (NLT) © 2007

The Holy Bible, King James Version (KJV) © 2003

The Holy Bible, English Standard Version (ESV) © 2001

The Holy Bible, God's Word ® Translation © 1995

The Bible Heart, from http://www.bibletruths.net/Archives/BTAR137.htm

What is the Heart, from http://www.nhlbi.nih.gov/health/health-topics/topics/hhw/

ABOUT THE AUTHOR

Dr. Raymond Findlater was born on the beautiful Caribbean Island of Jamaica. He emigrated to the United States of America in 1971 to pursue higher education. Although he professed faith in Christ as a child and experienced water baptism at age twelve, the young man had lost his way for many years but like the Prodigal Son, he has rededicated his life to Christ with complete surrender. His journey over the years has taken him through thirty-eight years of marriage to the same woman, fatherhood, service in the U. S. Air Force (twenty-six years of active and reserve duty), a stint as an adjunct instructor at Victor Valley College in San Bernardino County, California, and other varied and sundry odd jobs.

Dr. Findlater has been an educator with the School District of Osceola County Florida since 1997. During his struggle to complete his doctoral degree, Dr. Findlater made a promise to the Lord that if he were to complete the program successfully, he would dedicate the rest of his life to study, teach, and preach the gospel. So, true to his word and armed with a doctorate of education in educational leadership, he began sharing his morning and nightly devotions on a popular social media site with family and friends across several continents. His first book, *Victory through Surrender*, was conceived after friends and family requested a compilation of some of his postings.